FIRST AND LAST LOVES

JOHN BETJEMAN

✳

FIRST
AND LAST
LOVES

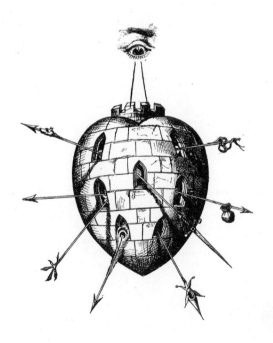

JOHN MURRAY
50 ALBEMARLE ST., LONDON, W.1

First published 1952
This edition 1969

Printed in Great Britain by
Latimer Trend & Co. Ltd., Whitstable
7195   1891   1

Dedicated
to the memory of
GERALD HAYNES
Schoolmaster of Lynam's, Oxford,
who first opened my eyes
to architecture

ACKNOWLEDGMENTS

I AM greatly indebted to Myfanwy Piper for making this collection of essays and talks about architecture and places. She read through many pages of dead papers, yellowing typescripts and periodicals, and with her sure critical perception weeded out much that was topical, sentimental, journalistic, pretentious and dull. Even so she has left you with plenty to complain about. But that is my fault, not hers. On reading through the page proofs, I was horrified at the patronising way I have written about Sir Giles Gilbert Scott, some of whose work I am only just beginning to appreciate. I must explain too that the overlapping which occurs in the articles "Victorian Architecture" and the "Illustrated Notes" which follow was not an oversight. It was not possible to cut either without altering what little meaning they have. So readers should read one or the other, but not necessarily both.

I am very grateful to my friend Mr. Piper for doing the illustrations for the Nonconformist Chapels and for making a drawing of his lithograph of Cheltenham, both tasks specially undertaken for this book. The Editors of the *Architectural Review*, *Signature*, *The Studio*, *Vogue* and *World Review* kindly gave me permission to reprint certain articles. The Hogarth Press most generously let me reprint the whole of the rather dated piece "Antiquarian Prejudice". I am also indebted to Max Parrish Ltd., Denis Dobson Ltd., the Librarians of the B.B.C., the Curator of the Manx Museum, for permission and help. The following other individuals have also helped me: Mr. David Verey, Captain H. M. Raleigh, Miss Cregeen, Miss Eileen Molony, Mr. P. Morton Shand, Mr. Frederick Etchells, F.R.I.B.A., Sir Ninian Comper and many others who will I hope take this the only intimation of my sincere gratitude.

CONTENTS

✳

Contents

ILLUSTRATIONS

Love is Dead

ENGLAND though not yet so ugly as Northern France and Belgium, is very nearly so. The suburbs which once seemed to me so lovely with their freckled tennis girls and their youths in club blazers have spread so far in the wake of the motor car that there is little but suburb left. We are told that we live in the age of the common man. He would be better described as the suburban man. There is a refinement about him which pervades everything he touches and sees. His books are chosen for him by the librarians, his arguing is done for him by Brains Trusts, his dreams are realised for him in the cinema, his records are played for him by the B.B.C.; the walls of his rooms are in quiet pastel shades, he has cereals for breakfast, and he likes everything in moderation, be it beer, religion or tobacco. He has a wife, a motor car and a child. He is the Borough Engineer, the Listener, the Civil Servant, the Town Clerk, the Librarian, the Art Historian, the Income Tax Inspector. So long as he is not any sort of creative artist he can be assured of an income and a pension at the end. He collects facts as some collect stamps, and he abhors excess in colour, speech or decoration. He is not vulgar. He is not the common man, but the average man, which is far worse.

He is our ruler and he rules by committees. He gives us what most people want, and he believes that what is popular is what is best. He is the explanation of such phenomena as plastic tea-cups, Tizer, light ale, quizzes, mystery tours, cafeterias, discussion groups, Chapels of Unity, station announcers. At his best he is as lovable as Mr. Pooter, but he is no leader. He is the Lowest Common Multiple, not even the

Highest Common Factor. And we have put him in charge of us, whatever his political party at the moment.

His indifference to the look of things is catching. We discover it in our attitude to the horrors with which the delicate variety of our landscape has been afflicted. We accept without murmur the poles and wires with which the Ministry of Fuel and Power has strangled every village, because they bring electric light and telephones to those who have been without these inestimable benefits. We put up with the foully hideous concrete lamp-standards for which the Borough Engineer and the Ministry of Transport are jointly responsible—each playing off the other—because the corpse-light they spew over road and pavement makes it safer for kiddies to cross and easier for lorries to overtake one another round dangerous corners. We slice off old buildings, fell healthy trees, replace hedges with concrete posts and chain-link fencing, all in the name of "safety first" which is another phrase for "hurry past". We accept the collapse of the fabrics of our old churches, the thieving of lead and objects from them, the commandeering and butchering of our scenery by the services, the despoiling of landscaped parks and the abandonment to a fate worse than the workhouse of our country houses, because we are convinced we must save money. Money is even more important than health or road-widening, so it is obviously infinitely more important than something so indeterminate as beauty. He is a foolish man who in a letter to a paper, or at a local council meeting or in Parliament dares to plead for something because it is good to look at or well made. He is not merely a conservative. He is a crank. He is unpatriotic and prepared to sell the country for an invisible asset. We have ceased to use our eyes because we are so worried about money and illness. Beauty is invisible to us. We live in a right little, tight little clinic.

Oh come, come, Mr. Betjeman, aren't you allowing your eloquence to run away with you? Things are not so bad as you imagine. I doubt if there has ever been a time when the desire for culture has been so widespread among our menfolk and womenkind. The interest in ballet, in opera, in chamber music and documentary film is something phenomenal. Museums have never had better seasons, and even picture galleries are widely patronised. Then you must admit that in your field of architecture the government housing schemes, particularly for our rural dwellers, have shewn a taste and reticence unknown in the evil days of private speculation by the jerry builder.

I doubt whether this interest in culture is more than an expression of restlessness. It is reaching for something that cannot be explained in terms of economics. It is a desire for the unworldly. It is a search for religion and it is far smarter than Christianity. As for the taste and reticence of government control, it is certainly easier on the eye than the brutalities of the speculator. By looking only at well-laid out municipal estates and averting one's eyes from the acres of unimaginative modern housing, by forgetting those terrible pipe-dreams come true of thick-necked brutes with flashy cars, elderly blondes and television sets—those modernistic, Egyptian, beaux-arts and other façades of the new factories outside every large town, by ignoring all these and much more, it is possible to live in a fool's para-dise of imagined culture, a sort of Welwyn Garden City of the mind.

But look for a moment at what is really there, and the suburban man is before us again. The old High Street just peeps above the shop façades. The well-known chromium and black gloss, Burton the Tailor of Taste, Hepworth, Halford, Stone, Woolworth & Co., Samuel, Bata, The Fifty Shilling Tailor, the Co-op, have transformed what was once a country town with the characteristics of its county into a home from home for the suburbanite, the concrete standards adding the final touch. When the suburbanite leaves Wembley for Wells he finds that the High Street there is just like home, provided that he does not raise his eyes from the pavement to see the old windows and uneven roofs, or go so far off the beaten track as to wander down a side-alley and see the backs of the houses and their neglected Somerset craftsmanship. Enterprising brewers, backing culture for all they are worth, have

3

turned the old inns into "pubs" and "locals". They have made a virtue of the solemn drinking of their chemicals. They have had Izal and porcelain put in the gents, and made the bar similar to it, save that they have added little tables and a counter. Sawdust and oil lamp or engraved glass and gas light, all the subtle distinction between private, jug and bottle, public and saloon, are being merged into the cleanly classlessness of the road-house. The local crudely-painted inn sign is replaced by the standardised sign with the big brewer's name. And inside, the old photographs of local teams and the framed picture from *Pears' Annual* are put in the dust bin, the walls are painted a light biscuit colour and reproductions of favourite artists of a brewers' publicity board are hung in their place. Nationalised or not yet nationalised, the gradual suburbanisation of enterprise continues, the killing of local communities, the stamping out of local rivalries and the supplying of everything by lorry from industrial towns. By luxury coach and local bus the villages are drained of life. Jealous of the misery created by too much road transport, the railways are trying to standardise themselves too. Those colours by which we were wont to know the part of England we were in—red for Midland, brown for Great Western, grained oak for East Anglia, green for Southern—have disappeared. For the convenience of suburbanites who like everything uniform and call it Administration, the trains are one of two colours.

Oh prams on concrete balconies, what will your children see? Oh white and antiseptic life in school and home and clinic, oh soul-destroying job with handy pension, oh loveless life of safe monotony, why were you created?

I see the woman with a scarf twisted round her hair and a cigarette in her mouth. She has put the tea tray down upon the file on which my future depends. I see the man on the chain-belt feeling tired, not screwing the final nuts. In a few months I see the engine falling out of the motor car. I see eight porters, two postmen and an inspector standing dazed for forty minutes on a provincial station, staring into space and waiting for what was once the Great Western which is now forty minutes late. I see those sharp-faced girls behind the buffet and the counter insulting the crowds who come to buy. Too bored to think, too proud to pray, too timid to leave what we are used to doing, we have shut ourselves behind our standard roses; we love ourselves only and our neighbours no longer. As for the Incarnation, that is a fairy story for the children, if we think it healthy for children to be told fairy stories. We prefer facts. They are presented to us by the thousand and we can choose those we like. History must not be written with bias, and both sides must be given, even if there is only one side. We know how many tons of coal are produced per week, how many man-hours there are in a pair of nylons, the exact date and the name of the architect and the style of a building. The Herr-Professor-Doktors are writing everything down for us, sometimes throwing in a little hurried pontificating too, so we need never bother to feel or think or see again. We can eat our Weetabix, catch the 8.48, read the sports column and die; for love is dead.

O Lord, who hast taught us that all our doings without charity are nothing worth; Send thy Holy Ghost, and pour into our hearts that most excellent gift of charity, the very bond of peace and of all virtues, without which whosoever liveth is counted dead before thee. Grant this for thine only Son Jesus Christ's sake. [BOOK OF COMMON PRAYER.]

The Mead,
    Wantage
April, 1952

5

1   WINTER AT HOME

N ow comes the time when gardeners have given up trying to sweep away leaves. We have taken the honesty out of the top shelf in the linen cupboard and stuck it in the brass altar vases of the village church. Last Sunday the last of the Michaelmas daisies were too frost-bitten to be conducive to public worship. Now England, having got rid of tourists and those who feel they must seek sunlight, settles down to be herself. With any luck there will be fogs in November and December so that the sky will not be poisoned with aeroplanes and a quiet of eternity will be about us, just the drip drip from wet branches and smells of wood-smoke and fungus in the lanes. The Women's Institute will take on new life with a revival of basket-making; more leather-work purses will be made than there is money to put in them; even Mrs. Hutchinson's talk on her visit to Rhodesia will seem interesting although the magic lantern is certain to fail.

Ah, the sweet prelude to an English winter! For me it is so much a more beautiful season than any other, which is just as well since it goes on for most of the year. It is a time when there is more colour in the country than there was ever before. Ploughed fields take on a look like a farming scene in the initial letter of a medieval manuscript. Bricks are an intenser red and Cotswold stone is more golden, the limestone and granite of the north is more silver, bare branches are like pressed seaweed against the pale blue sky. Whatever remains green is more deeply, richly green than it was before. This waiting, intense stillness is generally a prelude to a storm. The smallest sound is easily heard. Cocks are continually crowing, ducks quacking as though they were happy, and even across three miles of still, misty fields, it is possible to distinguish all six of the church bells as men practise method ringing in the oil-lit evening tower. But this night there is not one of those gigantic winter sunsets and the house is more than usually full of spiders, huge hairy ones which cast a shadow twice their own size on the drawing-room carpet. And then, in the night the storm begins. Will the trees stand it, this gale which makes them roar and creak and roar again? Will the earth ever be able to soak up these torrents which beat the house, brim the water-butts and swish on grass and gravel? And has anyone remembered to shut the upstairs window?

Winter is the one time when I feel I can indulge myself in reading what I like instead of what I ought to read. Time stretches out a little more and I stretch myself with it. Slow books come back and I try to forget our jerky modern novels. While the storm shakes the shutters, I re-read Scott, generally starting with *The Heart of Midlothian*. And as the great rumbling periods, as surely and steadily as a stage-coach, carry me back to Edinburgh, the most beautiful city in these islands, I feel an *embarras de richesse*. There is too much I want to read, too many memories I wish to experience.

Every winter I read *The Task* by William Cowper, and twice or thrice those wonderful books in it where he describes a Winter Evening, a Winter Morning and a Winter Walk at Noon. The frost blades of north Buckinghamshire, the snowed-over woodlands, the dog that gambolled in the snow, the bells and post horns, the cups of tea, melted, dead, silenced, evaporated for nearly two hundred years, come to life again. And if the next morning is nippy and white with frost, then Cowper's magic power of description gives an eternal look to the cold and sparkling scene so that even this duller landscape in which I live might be the gentle undulations round Cowper's Olney, Bucks, **or**

7

it might be something earlier still, a frost-bound Dutch landscape by Breughel.

Winter is the time for reading poetry and often I discover for myself some minor English poet, a country parson who on just such a night must have sat in his study and blown sand off lines like these, written in ink made of oak-gall:

> *Soon as eve closes, the loud-hooting owl*
> *That loves the turbulent and frosty night*
> *Perches aloft upon the rocking elm*
> *And hallooes to the moon.*

And here they are, these lines, widely spaced upon the printed page and hundreds more, by the Reverend James Hurdis, D.D., Incumbent of Bishopstone, Sussex, printed a century and a half ago, some of the most perfect descriptions of an English winter that were ever written in English. And you and I are probably the only people in England who are reading Hurdis. The smell of the old book is like a country church when first you open its door, the look of the pages is spacious like the age in which it was written and the broad margins isolate the poetry as Bishopstone must then have been isolated among windy miles of sheep-nibbled downs.

There is no need only to escape into the civilised past, which is more easily done in winter than in any other time of the year. Even modern barbarism becomes almost human, especially in places which make their money out of summer visitors. Am I wrong in thinking that the blonde with a handkerchief wound round her head and a cigarette in her mouth is a little politer now when she refuses to sell me the cigarettes I know she has in hundreds under the counter? Do I perceive a mood less casual in the bar-attendant at the Grand Hotel? Is it possible that when I ask for a room at the reception desk, I shall actually be accommodated instead of being sent away with a scornful refusal? Maybe this is all imagination. But of this I am quite certain, when I receive my fee for describing to you these joys of winter, I shall indulge in the greatest winter joy I know. I shall take the train to the coast and spend a night by the sea.

The train from London will be fairly empty. By the time evening has set in there will be hardly anyone in it at all, for the larger towns on the way to the sea will have taken off most of the passengers. What started as an express will have turned into a local train, stopping at oil-lit stations while the gale whistles in the ventilators of empty carriages. Standing out white on a blue glass ground, will appear the names of wayside stations and, reflected in a puddle, the light of a farmer's car in the yard will sparkle beyond the platform fence.

Then we will go on into the windy dark until at last there is a station slightly more important than those we have passed, lit with gas instead of oil, and that is mine. I shall hear the soft local accent, smell the salt in the wet and warmer air and descry through the lines of rain that lace the taxi's wind-screen, bulks of houses that were full and formidable in summer and now have not a light in any of their windows.

2   BOURNEMOUTH

BOURNEMOUTH is one of the few English towns one can safely call "her." With her head touching Christchurch and her toes turned towards the Dorset port of Poole she lies, a stately Victorian duchess, stretched along more than five miles of Hampshire coast. Her bed has sand for under-blanket and gravel for mattress and it is as uneven as a rough sea. What though this noble lady has lately disfigured her ample bosom with hideous pseudo-modern jewellery in the shape of glittering hotels in the Tel-Aviv style, her handsome form can stand such trashy adornment, for she is lovely still. Warm breezes caress her. She is heavy with the scent of *pinus laricio*, *pinus insignis*, the Scotch fir of orange-golden bark, the pinaster and black Austrian pine. She wears a large and wealthy coat of precious firs. Beneath it we may glimpse the flaming colours of her dress, the winding lengths of crimson rhododendron, the delicate embroidery of the flower beds of her numerous public gardens which change their colours with the seasons. The blue veins of her body are the asphalt paths meandering down her chines, among firs and sandy cliffs, her life-blood is the young and old who frequent them, the young running gaily up in beach shoes, the old wheeled steadily down in invalid chairs. Her voice is the twang of the tennis racket heard behind prunus in many a trim villa garden, the lap and roar of waves upon her sand and shingle, the strains of stringed instruments from the concert hall of her famous pavilion.

The sea is only one of the things about Bournemouth, and one of the least interesting. Bathing is safe. Sands are firm and sprinkled in places with shingle and in others with children. There are lines of bathing huts, bungalows and tents and deck chairs municipally owned, mostly above that long high water mark which hardly changes at all, for the tide at Bournemouth always seems to be high. Zig-zag paths, bordered by wind-slashed veronica, ascend those unspectacular slopes of sandy rock from Undercliffe to Overcliffe. From Undercliffe the lazy motorist may shout out of her motor-car window to her children on the beach, from Overcliffe she may survey the sweep of bay from Purbeck to the Needles, and, sickened by so much beauty, drink spirits in the sun lounge of one of those big hotels or blocks of flats which rise like polished teeth along the cliff top. The sea to Bournemouth is incidental, like the bathroom leading out of a grand hotel suite: something which is there because it ought to be, and used for hygienic reasons. Deep in a chine with its scent of resin and tap of palm leaves and plash of streamlets and moan of overhanging pine, an occasional whiff of ozone reminds us of the sea. But Bournemouth is mainly a residential town by the sea, not a seaside town full in summer only.

The inland suburbs of Bournemouth are like any other suburbs, indistinguishable from Wembley or the Great West Road. And they stretch for miles into Hants and Dorset, leaving here and there a barren patch of pylon-bisected heath. The main shopping streets have the usual ugly lengths of flashy chromium, though a pretty, early-Victorian stucco thoroughfare survives called the Arcade. The public buildings are less blatant and alien looking than the latest blocks of flats and hotels. But the beauty of Bournemouth consists in three things, her layout, her larger villas and her churches. All of these are Victorian.

Earliest Bournemouth is on the western and Branksome side of the Bourne which runs into the sea by the Pavilion. It consists of a few villas built by Mr. Lewis Tregonwell whose name survives in a terrace and a road and whose house was part of the Exeter Hotel. He started building in 1810. In 1836 a local landlord, Sir George Tapps of Westover and Hinton Admiral, built on the eastern bank of the stream.

Adding Gervis to his name, he went on building and called in Benjamin Ferrey, the Gothic church architect and friend of Pugin, to lay out his estate. Thus Gervis Place arose with its stucco Tudor-style villas. Tudor or Italian, the villas were varied, well spaced in their setting, roads were broad and planted with trees, but everything had to wind. Nothing was to be regular. That is why there is no formal promenade in Bournemouth and why there have always been so many footpaths and curving roads in the older and finer parts of the town. The place was carefully planned from its beginnings on the principle that nature abhors a straight line, the picturesque school of Georgian gardening surviving into Victorian times. This sense that Bournemouth is a garden with houses in it survived the century. The name Tapps-Gervis increased to Tapps-Gervis-Meyrick, hence Meyrick Avenue, Meyrick Park, Meyrick Road. And if you are not sure of the owner of the road, you may often guess its date from its name—Adelaide, Alma, Gladstone. They are hidden behind trees and flowering shrubs, down lengths of gravel bordered with rhododendron, these Victorian villas. Some are hotels, some are now government offices. They reflect every phase of leisured Victorian and Edwardian life—here a hint of Madeira, there an Elizabethan cottage, then an Italian villa like the Royal Bath Hotel. All these are in stucco and not later than the 'seventies. Then brick came in and we have "Flemish style" buildings, with gables and white wood balconies and leaded panes, of which J. D. Sedding's Vicarage at St. Clements and big house at the top of Boscombe Chine, called The Knole, are beautiful, satisfying examples. They look stately and practical. Later, a brilliant local architect, Sidney Tugwell, designed villas in the new art style with tiny windows fluttering cheerful chintz, low-pitched roofs of local stone and broad eaves—wholesome and simple buildings like home-made cakes. He had his imitators. And each of these strongly individual Victorian houses, not content with its garden-like road, Knyveton Road, Manor Road, Alum Chine or further inland round Meyrick

Park, has, or once had, a beautiful garden of its own. So that the real Bournemouth is all pines and pines and pines and flowering shrubs, lawns, begonias, azaleas, bird-song, dance tunes, the plung of the racket and creak of the basket chair.

Lastly the churches have the colour and clearness of the town. I doubt if any place in Britain has finer modern churches than Bournemouth and, what is more, they are all open and all alive. I visited fourteen of them on one week-day and found them all clean and cared for and in most of them people at prayer. Excluding Parkstone with its beautiful St. Peter's and the lovely Basilica of St. Osmund I thought the finest Bournemouth church was St. Stephen's in the centre of the town—designed by J. L. Pearson. It is worth travelling 200 miles and being sick in the coach to have seen the inside of this many-vistaed church, all in clean cream-coloured stone, with arch cutting arch, a lofty hall of stone vaulting providing view after view as you walk round it, each lovelier than the next and worthy of a vast cathedral. Away in the suburbs there is much that is beautiful, J. D. Sedding's famous church of St. Clement, scholarly and West-country looking in stone; Sir Giles Gilbert Scott's little Roman Catholic Church of the Annunciation, a brilliantly original design in brick, his first work after Liverpool Cathedral; St. Francis' church by J. Harold Gibbons on a new building estate, white, Italianate and vast. As the day drew to an end I entered a red-brick church in a hard red-brick shopping street at the back of Boscombe. St. Mary's, Boscombe, built about 1920. Here, out of the noise of the street, was a white, cool and spacious interior, friendly, beautiful, with golden screens and gold and blue east windows, gaily painted roofs and wide and high West-country arches. Clean and white and cheerful, the perfect seaside church. That last experience seemed to typify Bournemouth. You arrive tired from a long journey, you first see only the car parks, buses and jazzy blocks of flats and hotels. You turn into a side road and all is colour, light and life.

13

3　CHELTENHAM

BOOK ILLUSTRATION can colour a whole town or county. Who can look at a Cotswold manor, the distinct stones, the hollyhock spire, the clipped box, without running his gaze down the flagstones to the bottom right-hand corner where he will expect to find, written on a scroll among the snapdragon, F. L. GRIGGS? Who does not see in Merrion Square or Henrietta Street the Guinness-brown brick, the green, etched-in ironwork, the silver-grey stone of a Malton aquatint? Nor can I help associating the uneven silhouette of the Old Town at Edinburgh with a steel engraving of the 'thirties, while the diminishing terraces of its New Town remind me of more engravings in Thos. H. Shepherd's *Modern Athens*. The tumbled cottage by the sandy road, the flaming sunset behind the dumpy spire, the tree-surrounded ponds of southern Surrey can still recall Birket Foster's wood engravings. The red Dutch cliffs of Willet-land look well in pen and wash, vignetted for the 'nineties and the earliest half-tone illustrations. The cover of the *Strand Magazine* once made the Strand look beautiful, while its pages heightened the romance of Norwood, Brixton and Harrow Weald with its illustrations to *Sherlock Holmes*. Cheltenham comes from Ackermann's *Repository of the Arts* and continues into those lithographed architectural books of the 'forties and 'fifties.

Here is the relative increase of Cheltenham from when the Spa first became popular.

Census when taken	Number of inhabitants	Number of houses
1801	3,076	710
1811	8,325	1,556
1821	13,388	2,411
1831	22,942	5,000
1841	31,379	5,653
1851	35,062	7,365

We may put down the popularity of Cheltenham not merely to the fact that George III tasted the water—George III tasted almost as many Spa waters as has the author himself—nor merely to the visit of the Duke of Wellington, which seems to have been a success. We may put it down to liver trouble contracted in the East, for which the Cheltenham waters were long recommended as a cure. The properties of the water naturally attracted the military, so that a glance at the statistics printed above will also serve as an indication of the increase of Empire during the nineteenth century. Cheltenham now covers eight square, tree-shaded miles.

From many quiet houses in the midst of carefully tended gardens, blue eyes look out across the silver birches and see the Himalaya mountains above the stucco chimneys, or, looking at the lily-pond, dream again of Cashmere, until the temple gong in the hall calls the time for dressing and the single bell of a Low Church reminds us that there is a weekday evening prayer meeting somewhere. And bells and shouts from Cheltenham College bring back our youth, for Cheltenham is a military school, and from it Adam Lindsay Gordon went out to Australia never to return, except between the boards of one of the *Oxford Poets*. But many a distinguished Colonel and many a General has come back to the town of his old school, and so the links of Empire have held fast, and a man may sip his glass of Lansdowne (or sodium sulphate saline) within hearing of the smack of King Willow against the leather on the playing field of his old school.

The beauty of Cheltenham has been preserved almost entirely by the military [1]; and there is an absence of municipal swagger such as is to be found in a stock-broking, commercial town like Brighton. Lace curtains are only now disappearing from the windows, since the Colonel's daughter has been to the Slade; old-fashioned shops still exist. Bootmakers have discreet window displays. Chemists are still pharmaceutical and their shops have still those large bottles in the windows and a multitude of lettered coffers round the walls : there is a shop in Cheltenham which especially deals in ladies' hats of a size large enough to contain a mountain of coiled white hair.

The earliest Cheltenham architecture just comes into the copper engravings of the late eighteenth-century antiquity book. It is the Parish Church, to which most guide books desperately draw attention, beginning in ardent detail on every medieval feature, however much it has been scraped and renewed. But the Parish Church, though its origin may have been in the twelfth century, shows so much of the late nineteenth and early twentieth, that all its texture, delicacy, original arrangement and proportion have disappeared. It is a wood engraving from Brandon.

The first great period of Cheltenham is of the Ackermann's Repository date. It is possible in Cheltenham, on a sunny spring day, to see Greek revival architecture exactly as it looks in a coloured aquatint. There are the chestnut, the copper beech, the silver birch, the single Scotch fir embosoming the bright stucco house, be it Greek or Perpendicular, Soane or Salvin. The roof is purple-blue and with a low pitch, running to broad eaves under which sharp, engraved shadows fall deep down the bright yellow wall. Probably the house has little external decoration beyond a singularly delicate ironwork veranda painted green. Be the house Gothic or Moorish, Cheltenham ironwork is almost always Greek in design and painted green. In front of the house a sweep of golden gravel among green lawns furnishes a foreground to the aquatint.

Since this was written the Cheltenham Regency Society has been founded.

How appropriate, then, that much of Cheltenham's aquatint architecture should be by J. B. Papworth whose plates of ornamental architecture are a regular feature of the Repository. J. B. Papworth (1775-1847) designed the Rotunda (now pitiably neglected) in 1826, Lansdowne Place and various houses to the south of the High Street. He was at home in all styles, as his aquatints show, and many of his drawings are in the R.I.B.A. Library. Another Cheltenham architect of the aquatint period G. A. Underwood, who was a pupil of Soane from 1807 to 1815, designed the church in Portland Street, the Masonic Hall and many chaste Greek villas. There is a Soanean simplicity about a row of two-storey houses in Prestbury Road which suggests Underwood's work; Greek villas in the Park and various terraces to the south of the High Street may well have been his. Underwood's contemporary was J. B. Forbes, who designed the superb Pump Room on the Pittville Estate in 1825. This is an Ionic composition round a large domed hall. Its exterior was recently mutilated by some municipal department which destroyed the statues with which it was adorned.

From 1830, Cheltenham architecture sheers off the aquatint into the steel engraving. The decorator steps in as architect. The Queen's Hotel by R. W. and C. Jearrad (1838) has a façade which forms a terminus to the leafy Promenade, Cheltenham's smartest street. This façade is a magnificent stucco composition, original, bold, gay, decorated with coloured crowns and has, as its central feature, a row of Corinthian columns. At first glance the façade is chaste, correct, and a superb termination to the Promenade. The effect is as of a steel engraving in a local guide, a little unlikely but beautiful. Then examining the detail one sees that the columns have been engraved in not quite the right proportions, that there is something wrong about the depth of an entablature, that the building seems to be out of perspective. The Queen's Hotel has this quality of a steel engraving. Its architecture is not quite correct, but it is, none the less, effective.

Christ Church was designed by R. W. Jearrad, one of the designers of the Queen's Hotel, in 1837. It is one of the most successful buildings in Cheltenham externally, but it is wildly incorrect, vaguely Gothic, and with stupendous proportions all its own. One feels that F. Jearrad had some large book of antiquarian engravings, drawn to scale, of Magdalen College Tower, Oxford. He then had the enormous pinnacles on that tower reproduced according to the scale given in his book and stuck them on to Christ Church one hundred feet lower than they are at Magdalen. Pleased with the effect he added some more pinnacles a little higher up and, boldly forgetting the years between, he included some Early English lancet windows in the intervening surfaces and invented some Early English church doors. To crown this dreamlike base, all deep shadows and aspiring pinnacles, he added a graceful tower. The effect is romantic in the extreme, and so startling that I would travel one hundred miles to be startled so pleasantly. Unlike much romantic architecture of the time, Mr. Jearrad's Christ Church has a three-dimensional quality.

Let us capture for a moment the rapturous appreciation of Cheltenham in the past. First—a description of the Park, an elegant neighbourhood of detached stucco villas in the Greek, Italian, Swiss and Tudor styles laid out by Mr. T. Billings. "The sheltering trees on each side of the walk render it impervious to the rude embrace of Æolus; or the burning Phœbus. There is a sweet mellow beauty in this spot, which must render it highly congenial for the poet's mental compositions and to the nerves of the sensitive invalid." And now let us look inside the old Assembly Rooms. "Several chandeliers hang midway in the air, and their glittering drops vie with 'the light of the ladies' eyes' . . . there the wistful lookers-on will observe, that loving eyes and melting music conspire more to make hearts flutter, than does the graceful glide of the dance. But lo! a table full of fairy-like condiments in the opposite room, beckons the sylphs to refresh themselves by sedative and cooling draughts."[1]

The book from which these quotations come shows that Cheltenham was still progressing in the 'fifties. "New buildings are constantly and quickly appearing in Cheltenham; they rise as if a *magic wand* touched this lovely portion of our 'mother earth,' and bid it 'increase and multiply.'" The book is printed in blue ink, with ruled margins and steel engravings.

A playful battle of the styles occurred. Alongside the romantic architecture of the Jearrad brothers, who were primarily interior decorators, alongside the sketchy steel engravings was the sterner lithographic side. The Italian style was in. Those lithographs, faintly tinted with yellow and blue, depicting Italian villas by Lake Como or in St. John's Wood, were adapted to the stucco of Cheltenham. Their towers rise above cedars and their terraces are in a bold Anglo-Italian style of which the best is part of the Cheltenham Ladies' College in Bayshill Road. Such architecture belongs to the 'forties, 'fifties and 'sixties.

The battle of the styles in Cheltenham is gay. There is none of the heaviness of Pimlico or Earl's Court, because there has always been room to play about, and the Cheltenham waters seem to have had a loosening effect on her architects. The battle is gay, and the stone or stucco Victories, for Gothic, Swiss, Italian, Greek or Oriental, are rarely gimcrack or mere façadism. Perhaps the military clients insisted on thoroughness. Perhaps a conservative tradition in the town forbade the modern skimping of details. Certainly a tradition of spacious street planning lingered in Cheltenham until 1914. Here and there are Midland glazed bricks and municipal excursions into Edwardian Baroque, but there is still a certain wideness, except in the High Street, whose decent face has been smeared with commercialism. Everywhere else you will find the best and the most old-fashioned of architectural styles.

[1] Bailey's *New Hand-Book for Cheltenham* (Cheltenham, 1855).

A Cheltenham Regency Society has been founded just in time to save this lovely town from careerist civil servants and greedy speculators. If the harm that has been done in Cheltenham goes no further, in ten years Cheltenham will be as admired as Bath, and personally I think it is a gayer, more original town, with even more to admire. It is a bookshelf of aquatints, steel engravings and lithographs of the nineteenth century, ranged out in a Cotswold valley for all bibliophiles to see.

Pensions become reduced, colonels die, families go out to Kenya, and prefer London to the provinces when they return, but the great houses grow no smaller and the domestic service problem grows greater.

The lonely widows of military men are driven to Cheltenham hotels, where they wait, knitting sadly in the lounge and talking to visitors. Once a week a great grandson or great grand-daughter comes to tea from one of Cheltenham's numerous schools. And there is another week of watching the light in the chestnuts on the Promenade, walking in the Pittville Gardens, morning coffee at Kunzle's and back to an *en pension* lunch. There is less and less hope of the military holding out in the battle to save Cheltenham from "progress." The æsthetes must help them.

4 ABERDEEN GRANITE

MOST of us know successful Lowland Scots. Products of the manse and emancipation, they come to England and work their way up to the high administrative posts in Government Offices and Universities. Where organising ability, knowledge of finance, hard work and disinterested "service" to the "community" are required (to be rewarded with a not extravagant salary but eventually a pension and a decoration), where such careers are open, there you will find the Lowland Scots. Hard, logical, calmly energetic, they are the reverse of flibbertigibbets. Naturally such an abstract-minded people excels in architecture, the severest—I had almost said the most abstract—of the visual arts. Compare the average Italian church of the eighteenth century with a public building of the same time in Edinburgh. A rich façade greets your eye in Italy, a rich façade, alas, stuck on to the front of the church as though it were nothing to do with the building behind it. Now gaze at a Scottish bank or kirk or hall of the same date. The architecture goes all round the four sides, the decoration is sparse. What there is in the form of simple mouldings or low relief is essential only to emphasise the lines of construction. Scottish architecture is the hard logic of the theological Scot in the hard stone of Scotland. It is the energy of the organising, thorough and patient Lowlander translated into a visual style. You will see it even in medieval work. St. Mungo's Cathedral, Glasgow, is severer even than the severe Cistercian buildings of England like Fountains Abbey. Moulding, proportion, construction, no flowing carving, no fal-diddles—because of its thoughtful simplicity

I find Glasgow Cathedral the most satisfying medieval cathedral in these islands, its severe serenity is alarming.

Then suddenly, as though he said to himself, "I can't stand this restraint any more," the Scottish architect goes mad and produces something more wildly exuberant, more ornate and peculiar than anything to be found in England. Roslyn chapel, for instance, is a late medieval building which so flowers with carving, pendants and unbelievable riches of decoration that you might almost consider it to be a Burmese temple, were you not certain you had come out in a bus on a short journey from Edinburgh. Even in the Presbyterian kirks, the Victorian Scots sometimes let themselves go. All may be plain within, covenant-keeping fittings, bare table, towering pulpit, plain glass, grim walls and rising rows of sermon-centred pews, but suddenly the architect has said, "You may restrain me inside the kirk, but you wait till I get outside," and all the marbles of the cliffs of Scotland will be jammed on to the front and a steeple will be built of such fantastic richness that, except for an absence of Christian symbolism in the form of cross or statued saint, it might have been conceived by the Pope of Rome himself. I think particularly of the steeple of a Presbyterian kirk at Queen's Cross, Aberdeen. I never saw such a thing. I cannot describe its style or changing shapes as it descends in lengthening stages of silver-grey granite from the pale blue sky to the solid prosperity of its leafy suburban setting. I only know that when I tried to draw this late Victorian steeple, I gave it up at the seventh attempt. It is this mixture of the romantic and the severe that makes Scottish architecture so exciting.

It was this anticipation of treats for the eye that drew me to Aberdeen. For even in Lowland Edinburgh there are contrasts enough. Edinburgh, that most beautiful of all the capitals of Europe, no, not excepting Rome—Edinburgh though it produced John Stuart Mill, also, thank God, gave birth to Sir Walter Scott. If Edinburgh can thrill with contrasts what, I thought, may I not expect to find in

Aberdeen?—I did not know whether the Lowland Scottish genius for architecture had a Highland counterpart.

James Gibbs, the Adam Brothers, Colin Campbell, James Stuart, "Capability Brown," Sir William Tite, Thompson, Gibson—these are only some of the names of Classic architects who have come from Scotland to embellish England with their buildings. Inevitably many Scots became civil engineers when that science divorced itself from architecture, and the famous names of Nimmo, the Stevensons and the Rennies are among the first. For, naturally, engineering made a strong appeal to the Scottish mind, so attracted by fundamental structural principles in building.

In the south we think of Aberdeen granite as that highly polished pink stuff which flushes the white cheeks of Metropolitan cemeteries and forms glistening shafts to Gothic Revival façades. But the granite which comes from the immediate neighbourhood of Aberdeen is grey and silver, a lovely stone, immensely durable and worked with consummate skill in the deep, shadowy quarries. The pink granite comes chiefly from Peterhead, thirty miles north of the city, and from the Island of Mull on the other side of Scotland. No one can go to Aberdeen and not become interested in granite. I shall not forget my amazement, taking the tramcar one windy day down to the sea beach for the first time and standing on a lonely shore below the tufted links which separate Aberdeen from the sea. All around me was the veined and glittering produce of the cliffs of Scotland pounded into rounds and ovals by resistless breakers. So beautiful, so varied were the stones on the beach, grey, silver, pink, red, crimson, white, green, purple, pink-red, and silver again, that for a moment it was like standing in a dream of avarice surrounded by precious stones. And then, on the tide line where the waves had washed the pebbles so that they were still wet, they glowed with an intenser colour just as the city of Aberdeen glows a deeper, richer silver after rain. I collected fifteen different sorts of granite in as many minutes.

Granite is the strongest building stone in these islands, the hardest to shatter and the hardest to work. So hard is it that joints are hardly perceptible and a great column in such granite can be made to appear as a solid unjointed block.

The granite called me to Aberdeen; that it was Highland and I know only Lowlands also called me, and so did the thought that the city was the birthplace of James Gibbs, the great architect of the eighteenth century, and J. N. Comper, the great church architect of today. But there was another reason for going—the excitement of seeing a place I had never visited before. I bought guides of all sorts in one of the many marvellous second-hand-book shops of Edinburgh, for old books about Aberdeen are cheap in Edinburgh and vice versa. Finally I bought a modern one so as to see what the city looked like today: there were usual photographs of crowded commercial streets, draughty promenades, bandstands and putting greens.

From Waverley Station north and north for hours. I had not realised there was so much Scotland. The train ran on, over wide brown moors with bluely distant inland mountains and then along the edges of cliffs whose grass was a deep pre-Raphaelite green. And down steep crevices I saw rocks and fishermen's cottages above them, but still no Aberdeen. Could there be such a thing as a great city with tramcars, electric lights, hotels, and cathedrals so far away among empty fields, so near the North Pole as we were going? In England, spring had brought the leaves out on the trees, but here the wind-swept beechwoods were bare and daffodils and primroses were freshly yellow on brown woody banks that sloped to browner, tumbling streams. And then the line curved and objects familiar to me from my guide-book illustrations came to view.

Here was I, a filthy Saxon, alone at last in Aberdeen. My hotel had a plain grey granite front contrasting with the brown jazz-modern of its interior. I was in Aberdeen, but in this slick lounge with its leatherette and walls of empire wood and sub-Brangwyn decorations.

I might just as well have been in Manchester, in Leeds or Salt Lake City. This is progress. This is inter-nationalism.

You can never enjoy the beauty of a Western city in its shopping streets. The multiple stores which affront the dignity of Aberdeen are no less offensive than their brothers shouting out among the now unlovely buildings in Princes Street of Edinburgh. My hotel, where old-fashioned cleanliness and comfort contrasted unexpectedly with its jazzy decorations, was in the shopping area. I would have to turn down side streets to see the real Aberdeen.

There are three periods of building in Aberdeen—the medieval, the early nineteenth century and the modern.

Away down the tramlines to the north, surrounded by new granite housing estates at a decent distance and on a rise above the beech-bordered meadowland of a river, stands Old Aberdeen, which has a Cathedral, a University and some Georgian houses, built of huge blocks of granite, a strange-textured place with an atmosphere of medieval and Jacobite grandeur about it, a place that really makes you feel you are in the Northernmost seat of learning, so remote, so windswept and of such a solid, grey strangeness. Here is the old King's College of Aberdeen University and here is its chapel with a low tower from which spring ribs that support a Renaissance style crown. St. Giles' Edinburgh and St. Nicholas' Newcastle and St. Dunstan's-in-the-East London have similar spired adornments. But none of these is so satisfactory as that of Aberdeen. Inside, this chapel is remarkable for its canopied stalls in dark oak, the only medieval church woodwork surviving complete in Scotland after the ravages of Knox. It is not at all like the lace-like soaring of the East Anglian woodwork, it is squat and square and rich with inventive designs through which trail wooden thistles. And to the solid archi-tecture, designed for resisting storms and simply designed because of the hardness of the granite from which it is made, the elaboration of this woodwork is a perfect contrast. Finally there are windows, like the rest of the chapel very early sixteenth century, of a style so curious and original as to be unlike any Gothic outside Scotland. The buttresses run up through the middle of the tracery and the arches of all the windows are round.

Not far from King's Chapel is St. Machar's strange Cathedral. The west end is the thing to see; seven tall lancets of equal height flanked by square towers with no openings, and on top of each tower a dumpy spire in a style half Gothic, half Renaissance. The interior has been stripped of its plaster and ancient furnishings, except for a wooden roof of some richness, too high and dark to be visible, so that the effect of the building inside is merely one of size.

You cannot walk back and down the main streets of Aberdeen proper (as opposed to Old Aberdeen) without being aware of the noble planning of late Georgian times: wide streets, such as Union Street, stately groups of grey granite buildings in a Grecian style, crescents on hill tops and squares behind them. These are largely the work of two architects, friendly rivals, John Smith the City Architect and Archibald Simpson. Smith was, I think, the less interesting of the two. He built in correct classic and fifteenth-century style and with granite, close-picked and single-axed so that it was tamed to carry almost as much carving of capitals and mouldings as a softer building stone. A lovely screen in Union Street, rather like that at Hyde Park Corner, is his and many a handsome classic and English Perpendicular style public building.

But the original genius is Archibald Simpson. At the start of my visit my attention was held by a huge wall of granite, so bold, so simple in design, so colossal in its proportions that I stood puzzled. I have seen nothing like it before or since. Egyptian? Greek? Eighteenth century? Modern? No, it couldn't be modern, for see the granite is weathered. This was the New Market built by Archibald Simpson in 1842. The magnificence of the entrance is designed to show the strength and quality of granite: the architect realised that there was no point in carving this unyielding material into delicate detail. Let the stone speak for itself and then emphasise its scale and texture by a few strong mouldings and broad pilasters projecting only an inch or two from the face of the building. The inside of this covered market is worthy of its outside—colossal, simple, constructional. I seemed to be stepping into one of those many-vistaed engravings by Piranesi. It was a great oblong hall with curved ends and all around a row of plain circular-headed arches rising to the glass and timber roof. Half-way down the wall height ran a gallery of shops. Shafts of sunlight slanted through the arches on to the wooden shops and stalls of the central space and the surrounding gallery. Archibald Simpson: here was an architect of genius, a Soane, a Hawksmoor, someone head and shoulders above the men of his time. Simpson's work is almost always of the kind that depends on proportion for its ornament. His two-storey houses in crescents, Bon Accord and Marine Terraces for instance, are very plain but have all the subtlety in the glazing bars, now alas too often destroyed in favour of plate glass. But his greatest work is a brick tower and spire opposite the Art Gallery. The fact that it is in red brick makes it stand out, but not glaringly, among the grey granite of the rest of the city. It must have looked more wonderful still when the lead spires, for which Aberdeen was famous, were making further contrast. How can I explain why this tall plain spire is so marvellous that only Salisbury is in my opinion its rival? I think it is because of the way it grows out of the high, thin-buttressed tower below it, because of the pinnacles and tall gables at its base, because its very plainness is so carefully considered. It was designed in 1844 long before any architect had succeeded in 'creating' in the Gothic style on Gothic principles of construction—all other architects were only imitating at that time.

When looking at the work of the present century no one can dismiss Marischal College, Aberdeen. Wedged behind the huge Town Hall, in an expensive and attractive mid-Victorian baronial style, I saw a cluster of silver-white pinnacles. I turned down a lane towards them, the front broadened out. Bigger than any cathedral, tower on tower, forests of pinnacles, a group of palatial buildings rivalled only by the Houses of Parliament at Westminster—the famous Marischal College. Imagine the Victoria tower with a spire on top, and all that well-grouped architecture below of lesser towers and lines of pinnacles executed in the hardest white Kemnay granite looking out over the grey-green North Sea, and you have some idea of the first impression this gigantic building creates. It rises on top of a simple Gothic one designed by Simpson in 1840. But all these spires and towers and pinnacles are the work of this century and were designed by Sir Alexander Marshall Mackenzie. You have to see them to believe them. True, they do not bear close inspection. The hollow central tower reveals a brick core within to support its spire. The inside seems small after all this outward magnificence—but as a piece of architectural showmanship, Marischal College is fine, an equivalent of Sir George Oatley's soaring University Tower at Bristol.

Aberdeen's best modern building I have left to the last. It is the addition to St. Andrew's Episcopal Cathedral by J. N. Comper, an Aberdonian who has already done much distinguished work in the city. You go in by a rather dingy entrance to a flat Perpendicular-style building designed by Simpson in 1816, when he was a man of twenty-six. You push open the door and your heart gives a leap—there, stretching away as in an old Dutch oil-painting, is Comper's superb renovation of the interior. White arcades by Simpson, in a simple style with big mouldings, lead to a great double-aisled east end which Comper added in a style perfectly blending with the older building. White plaster vaulting diminishes away in perspective adorned with baroque gold and coloured shields. And there, far at the east end, is a great baldachin over the altar in burnished gold with a gold spire like that on King's Chapel. And beyond the gold of the baldachin, intensely gold in this blazing whiteness, you see the deep blue tints, the green and the red of Comper's large east window.

I have only briefly sketched some of the glories of Aberdeen—there in those miles of Highland where the Dee comes falling from the conifer forests of John Smith's castle at Balmoral. In the words of a little-known Victorian poet,

> *Farewell Aberdeen 'twixt the Donside and Deeside*
> *How oft have I strayed through the long summer day*
> *On the fringe of the links o'er thy wide-spreading seaside*
> *To see the pink pebbles caressed by the spray.*
> *How gay as a student by King's rugged steeple*
> *I loitered in archways and meadowpaths green*
> *To my Jacobite sympathies kind were the people*
> *Though deep in Balmoral dwelt Hanover's Queen.*
>
> *From windows of dreamland I see thy grey granite*
> *All sparkling with diamonds after the rain,*
> *The Dee and the arch and suspensions that span it*
> *And fir-covered forests that rise from the plain.*
> *Down Union Street with majestical motion*
> *Electrical tramcars go painted in green,*
> *The ships to thy quaysides come in from the ocean*
> *I leave thee for ever, my loved Aberdeen.*

5　LEEDS—A CITY OF CONTRASTS[1]

BERNARD SHAW said something about Leeds—that it ought to be burned down, or words to that effect; expressed of course with more epigrammatic force and probably rather more kindly. And this is not surprising. Leeds is not a city for Mr. Shaw; it caters for communists and conservatives. An individualist would not understand it. So individualists have no right to criticise it. It is as though an art critic walking through a spinney were to object to the contours of a mound made by wood ants. The person to examine the heap should be the entomologist: the person who ought to examine Leeds should be the town planner. An æsthetic appreciation of Leeds is of little value, because Leeds has little use for æsthetics. For this reason the Civic Hall at Leeds must be regarded only as a symbol of the Civic Pride of the Conservative party in that city.

By likening Leeds to an ants' nest, I do not mean to decry the city or its inhabitants, but rather to show that Bernard Shaw went no deeper than an art critic.

To understand Leeds, to understand its Civic Hall and the regrettable Headrow, one must acquire a Leeds sense of proportion. And this is done by realising two things about Leeds. First, it is a Victorian city. Secondly, it is parochial. These two qualities are far more blessed than is generally supposed. Today, when cosmopolitanism is still the rage, parochialism, and all that goes with it, is unpopular. Leeds does not attract tourists. There is not even a

---

[1] 1933.

guide-book to the city. Life in Leeds must be unbearable for the Londoner.

Leeds is a Victorian city. Once the train passes Grantham the character of England changes; you enter a foreign country. Disused branch lines, now only sidings, are full of empty trucks labelled L.N.W.R., G. & S.W., N.B., G.N.R., M.R., memorials of happy days before the railways amalgamated. Even the large, gas-lit stations with their smoking-rooms, buffets, first-class, second-class and general waiting rooms, whose green sunless walls once sheltered varying degrees of commercial prosperity, are still plastered with notices belonging to the old railway companies. And when, here and there, some modernistic poster has been introduced on to black platform or into high secluded refreshment room, it is as though a woman with make-up had entered with harsh giggles and puffed cigarette smoke into that ordered Victorian life.

And outside the stations, from the high embankments the country spreads out like a map. Large mills, with square panes broken, stand up among strips of houses stretched around them, "TO LET," "THIS CONVENIENT FACTORY FOR SALE"; the owners of the old-established firms have gone bust or sold out and retired to simple cottages in the south, their large Italianate mansions in Woodhouse, Headingly and Allerton, once silent, wealthy suburbs, pulled down and the gardens chopped up into building estates. Meanwhile, the workmen have remained, living in rows of back-to-back houses around the factories and the mills because they cannot afford to live elsewhere, and hoping that some rich man will come and open again that gaunt and empty building which once brought them and their families a livelihood. And between the industrial communities, scattered in the southern suburbs between Wakefield and Leeds, are a few smoke-blackened farms, with paper-strewn pasturage, whose fences are gapped and footpaths well-trodden by the feet of the unemployed. And somehow in Leeds itself the rain seems always to be falling, gathered on the northern hills around the moors—the moors which not even streets and mills can shut out, reminders to the citizens of a hungry freedom beyond.

You leave the Great Northern Station and turn to the right down Wellington Street, and in no time you are in the City Square. It is just such a City Square as you would imagine Leeds would have. Alfred Drury's lamp standards, nudes representing *Night* and *Morning*, hold arc lamps, now fitted with drawn-wire bulbs. But nudity still shocks many of the inhabitants. The General Post Office, a large and vulgar affair; the Queen's Hotel, the Ritz of Leeds, with decorations by J. F. Bentley later to be architect of Westminster Cathedral; and some offices in Portland stone reminiscent of Oxford Street, flank all sides of the square save one, where still stands the Mill Hill Unitarian Chapel—the same chapel in which Priestley preached—an eighteen-forty reminder in black Protestant northern Gothic of the Nonconformist conscience which has made Leeds what it is. And, almost hidden, are the impressive, simple entrance piers to Wellington Station. Trams, trains and tricycle bells and gear changing—if these are the times, then Leeds moves with them.

Yet, what *were* the times of Leeds? If you walk a short distance from the City Square you will come to Park Square, a delightful eighteenth-century group with Brodrick's fine Town Hall (1858) rising up behind it, black above the pink brick of the earlier houses. And down by the brown waters of the Aire and Calder Canal you will still see only nineteenth-century mills and warehouses, whose undiversified and solid exteriors are the cathedrals of the industrial north. Beside them, the black, locked Protestant churches with their commodious galleries, Church of England baize and marble monuments to departed manufacturers, seem less like places of worship. "I can't recollect the time when I did not go to the factory. My father used to drag me there when I was quite a little fellow, in order to wind reels for him." [1]   Life centred round the factory all right, and God spake out from the pages of the Old Testament.   At the end of the eighteenth century the factories were placed at the east end of the town and the west end was residential.   Park Square, Hanover Square, Bedford Place and Queen Square became engulfed in the westward spread.

Let me first consider the nineteenth-century development of Leeds architecturally, for the social aspect must come under the heading of parochialism.   On airy Richmond Hill, at the east of the town, houses were built close up against the factories for the workers: rows of two-storeyed houses built back-to-back with no gardens at all and only the cobbled street and the houses opposite to look at.   Several families lived in each two-roomed house.   Go to the bottom of Nippet Lane and see what the old speculators did.   A man named Weller bought a small bit of ground.   On it he crammed as many houses as possible, running in straight lines off the main street;   Weller Avenue, Weller Grove, Weller Mount, Weller Place, Weller Terrace, Weller Road, Weller View.   Sometimes, with touching parental affection, he would bring his children in—Nellie Grove, Back Nellie Grove, Archie Street, Archie Place, Doris Crescent, Back Doris Crescent, or use long words—Stipendiary Street, Industrial Street, Back Cemetery Lane.   But the houses would be much the same, just as crowded, only a little more or a little less pretentious, according to their dates, and always among them, like the house of God, black mills and blacker chapels and churches.

So much for the industrial dwellings.   The main streets are different.   The Kirkgate and the Briggate, once plain shopping districts intersected by shambles, not unlike the streets of Cork or Limerick today, cast off their Georgian glory and assumed the Jacobean, the Romanesque, the Holbeinesque, the Early English, the Perpendicular and the neo-Georgian, in Leeds phorpres brick and stone and

[1] *The Heart of John Middleton*, Mrs. Gaskell (1850).

33

terra-cotta. If you wait, sheep-like, in the long queue for the Roundhay tram, you will see more of this, the other side of the picture. Grass appears, the houses spread out, they are higher, they are detached, some have turrets, some have towers, and the larger, finer ones have become municipal property. There was a time when Mr. Peter Fairbairn's house "Woodsley" was the most lavishly decorated in England. At that time Queen Victoria stayed in it to open Brodrick's Town Hall. *The Illustrated London News* shows her admiring a pair of vases, a bust and a portrait in the presence of the owner (later Sir Peter Fairbairn), who was Lord Mayor of Leeds. Those were the days! Melon à la Coburg, Saumon-Balmoral, Bœuf Victoria, Fraises (out of season) Albert Prince Consort, Champagne, Lemonade, Selzer, Claret, Burgundy, Punch. Sitting on a packing case in McConnel's wine shop you can still imagine it all, while old men who once sent sherry to the grand merchants' houses hand out double scotches to commercials.

It was in these great days of Leeds that Cuthbert Brodrick was given his opportunity. He built the Town Hall (by far the finest building in the city), the Corn Exchange, the Leeds Institute, the King Street Warehouses, and several private houses. It is unlikely that one whose tastes were for the monumental would have concerned himself with houses, but what Brodrick did accomplish is the best monument a Victorian industrial city can be expected to have, a sequence of noble public buildings in the grand classical manner, before it died down into contemporary blatancy of "naicenesses."

And now for Leeds parochialism. It is a long story based on temperament and surroundings. To take surroundings first. Leeds has a population of a little over 500,000. It is not a very over-crowded city, it is merely appallingly badly housed. On the deaths from tuberculosis, the infant mortality, and the results of compulsory constipation it is needless to expatiate. The City Council, however, is not without resourcefulness. Under the 1930 Act it decided on a five-year programme; 2,000 of the back-to-back houses were to be demolished in that time and an adequate number of houses erected to replace them. In the first two years of the plan twenty-five were demolished and 942 new ones built. At best it will take 190 years to clear the city of back-to-backs.

The crowded conditions in what Queen Victoria called "this great city" naturally make its poorer inhabitants aware of one another's lives. You *have* to know your neighbour opposite on the first floor when you want to string a clothes line across the street to dry your own washing. Each house has its doorsteps yellowed on the edges: thousands of people are content to wait in queues. Leeds is indeed an ants' nest. And when the King and Queen came in August, 1933, to open the new Civic Hall (quite forty houses must have been demolished to clear the site), some of the saddest, dingiest little lanes had their decorations and hardly an exhausted Wolf Cub or irritated infant was without its red, white and blue favour or Union Jack. I was wandering about in the little lanes of the Richmond Hill Ward (average 2.17 persons per room) as the guns went off which announced the Royal entrance to the city. The courts and alleys where I stood were deserted. Everyone had gone to see the King and Queen. Suddenly bells pealed out under the clouds and even louder than the bells came the cheering. When I approached as near to the centre as I could through the crowds, the sun came out and down the steps of the Town Hall came the Queen in white. The cheers were deafening, hats and flags were waved. The city was alight with excitement. And then when the rain fell in the evening, after the Royal visitors had driven away, back went the crowds to their back-to-backs, "Long Live the King, God Bless our King and Queen." "It is my earnest hope and prayer that today's ceremony may prove

[1] Today prefabs spread over the Leeds suburban areas. Quarry Hill Flats, a colossal fortress designed to induce the worker to improve his living conditions, has been turned into a slum.

35

the beginning of increased prosperity for this great city." That should be proof enough of Leeds loyalty. And like a loyal parish Leeds did not expose its blemishes that day. It smiled through its illness. I think a city which has such remarkable people should take better care of them.

The remarkable people are only one side of the picture. There is the University closely identified, unlike Oxford and Cambridge, with the city which gave it birth. Here the intellectual life of the north, which produced most engineers, philosophers and poets of nineteenth-century England, finds inadequate embodiment, though the new Parkinson building designed by T. A. Lodge will greatly increase the accommodation. There is also the other fifth of the population which rules the four-fifths. They are Yorkshire people too, and just as loyal and still parochial. If you go out to dinner with one of them up in Roundhay—"dinner is served between 5.30 and 7.30" throughout the town—you will get an insight into their lives. A comfortable semi-detached residence in the Tudor style will welcome you, for the days of detached mansions in their own grounds have passed. And there will be a look round the garden and the wireless after dinner, and talk about Leeds this and Leeds that: the Town Hall is the third longest in the world, the cloth output is the largest in the world, the Civic Hall is the most beautiful Civic Hall in the world.

And from this talk there naturally arises the question of new buildings. The best architects must be got for the best city. So Sir Reginald Blomfield, from London, designed the Headrow, a bold street cut with fine imagination and foresight right from the Town Hall to St. Peter's Street. The Headrow consists of shops with offices above them. The buildings are constructed of steel and subsequently ornamented with brick and Portland stone, the parapets being diversified by urns. The incline of the Headrow from Victoria Square to the Briggate is rather severe. Here the effect of the stepped roof lines is unpleasing, and there can be no denying that Sir Reginald's

36

architectural decoration does not look at home in homely Leeds. I found on enquiry that the Headrow was not popular. One can only wonder why the architect did not follow the early nineteenth-century industrial tradition of Leeds, of which there are plenty of examples in side streets and in old engravings and photographs, with Trinity Church as a good example of the use of local material.

But that is perhaps a personal matter. I went to Leeds to see the Civic Hall but there was no seeing the Civic Hall without seeing Leeds at the same time. One can understand why Mr. Vincent Harris was chosen as architect. He had designed the Sheffield Town Hall, and Leeds was not going to be outdone by Sheffield. A site was chosen near the Town Hall, but higher up, so that the new building was bound to dominate the old. Should it attempt to harmonise or give up the struggle? Mr. Vincent Harris is not a Brodrick; that he was in two minds as to what to do is as obvious as are the two steeples with which he terminated his main façade. The result is that the building, looked at with the Town Hall in the foreground, is out of place. The twin steeples are more elaborate than that on the Town Hall—they are a cross between St. Vedast's, Foster Lane, and St. John's, Waterloo Road—yet their effect is nullified by the older building. The plain returns and wings look well, but the portico, a necessary justification for twin steeples, mars the otherwise plain and harmonious front. There has been much adverse criticism of the building, particularly from those who have not seen it. But photographs have not done the building justice. The busy streets of Leeds are below. Two main ones almost converge on the building, so that as the sightseer wanders among the hotchpotch of commercial styles around Infirmary Street and the City Square, he suddenly catches a glimpse of one or other brilliant white steeple, rising above tram lines and turrets, terminating an otherwise dreary street. He never sees both steeples at once. What the effect will be when the Portland stone is blackened I cannot say. But I think the odd effect of a close view of the exterior is justified. For the style of the extra-ordinary gilded clocks I can see less justification. Yet the shrewdest remark of all came from a Yorkshire builder in the bar of the *Golden Cock* in Kirkgate. "The Civic Hall—you know what that is—a structure of steel; but the Town Hall—that's architecture, that's craftsmanship. It's *grown* up. There's no more steel in that than'ld make a lion's cage."

6 THE ISLE OF MAN

NOT long ago I stepped out of an Edwardian electric tram-car on
to the grassy height of Snaefell, two thousand feet above sea-
level. The day was clear and I could see Snowdon seventy-
three miles away to the south-west and, much nearer, the mountains
of Cumberland, the Mull of Galloway and, in the west, the mountains
of Mourne—four countries in bluish outline beneath a sky of mother-of-
pearl and a wrinkled sea all round us, cloud-patched with streaks of
purple.

Four countries seen from a fifth—this ancient kingdom of Man
which once owned the Sodor or southern islands of Scotland. The
tram-car returned down the mountainside. Many who had landed at
the top went into the café for tea or beer and I had, for a moment, the
whole island to myself, thirty-two miles long and twelve wide at my
feet; brown moorland and mountain in the middle with tiny fields on
the lower slopes, green slate and blue slate, silver limestone and red
sandstone, gorse and blaeberries and ling, gigantic cliffs and hidden,
wooded glens, foxgloves, fern and scabious on Cornish-looking hedges,
whitewashed cottages thatched with straw and drowned in fuchsia
bushes. It is a bit of Ulster set down in the sea, a bit of England,
Scotland, Wales and Cornwall too, a place as ancient as them all, a
separate country, Norse and Celtic at once.

The Isle of Man, like Shakespeare, has something memorable for
everyone. It is a place of strong contrasts and great variety. Yet in
southern England it is hardly known at all.

Yet from June to September half a million people cross from the coast of Lancashire, whole towns at a time. Then lodging houses are stuffed to capacity, then bathing things hang from the sixth floor downwards, then the main road round the island, the famous T.T. track, hums with "charas," and still there is room. Each time I have visited the Isle of Man it has been at the height of the season and each time I have been able to lose myself in the country. I have tramped knee-deep in blaeberry bushes on the wild west coast of the island, looking in vain for the ruins of a Celtic chapel and never seeing a soul till I turned inland and walked down rutty farm lanes between foxgloves and knapweed to the narrow-gauge railway. And on the same evening I have been able to lose myself again in the crowds on Douglas front, to see Norman Evans in variety at the Palace and afterwards to watch a thousand couples dance in one of the big halls. All this in so small a kingdom, such wildness and such sophistication, such oldness and such newness. The trams, the farms, the switchback railways, the mountain sheep, the fairy lights and the wood-smoke curing kippers —how can I cram them all in? The clearest way of describing the island is to divide it into the two peoples of which it consists, the Manx and the visitors.

And the Manx come first. When the last boat of holiday-makers has steamed out of Douglas harbour back to Lancashire, about fifty-thousand Manx are left behind: the Christians, Quayles, Crellins, Kewleys, Caines, Kermodes, Clucases, Kellys, Cregeens—Manx names seem almost all to begin with C, K or Q. They are a shy, poetical people. The look of their country is Celtic. There are smallholdings and plenty of *antiquities*, but not much ancient architecture. The island looks like Cornwall, Wales and Ireland mixed. But Man is Norse as well as Celtic. Until 1266 it belonged to Norway. Race enthusiasts see in the long, tall Manxmen with their fair hair and blue eyes and long moustaches, the descendants of the Vikings. Man was the capital of a Viking kingdom of islands, and very well the Vikings ran it and very slowly they adopted the Christian religion of the conquered Celts.   Then the Scots took it over and finally Edward III, the strong man of the time, made England overlord.   In 1405 Henry IV gave it to the Stanley family.   The Stanleys became not only Earls of Derby but Kings of Man.   And when that line of Stanleys died out, the kingship passed to a descendant, the Duke of Atholl.   Late in the eighteenth century Man was still an independent country, an unknown island of mists and cliffs and smugglers with a king who was usually non-resident.   Spain and France and Portugal shipped dutiable goods to Douglas and Castletown and other Manx ports.   Manx sailors would run specially designed fast ships to England.   By their own laws they were doing nothing illegal.   They were only breaking British laws.

The island was also a place of refuge for debtors at this time when, by the laws of England and Ireland, a person could still be imprisoned for debt.   I believe that Sir William Hillary, founder of the National Lifeboat Institution, who lived at Falcon Cliff, Douglas, was one of these debtors, though he did nothing but good to the Isle of Man.   On the other side of Douglas Bay the ruined rake "Buck Whaley" built himself Fort Anne, now an hotel, where, safe from his creditors, he wrote his memoirs.   He died in 1800.

Assuming much moral indignation about the smugglers and debtors who had settled on Man, as well as seeing that the island might be both profitable financially and useful in times of war, the British Government bought out the last claims of the Duke of Atholl to kingship of Man in 1828 for nearly half a million pounds.   This was an immense sum for the period, but the British Government gained in the long run.   The only people who did not do well out of this sale were the Manx.

He who has not seen the Tynwald on Tynwald Day does not know how ancient and independent Man is.   Of course the feel of another country is in the air as soon as one lands.   It is an island, it has generous licensing hours, it has its own flag of three armoured legs on a red background, its own language (half Scottish, half Northern-Irish Gaelic), its own customs in both senses of that word. But the full Manxness shines on July 5th, the annual holiday of Tynwald Day. The centre of the island is St. John's. Here most valleys meet and here surrounding mountains hide the sea. Carts from all the sheadings, tall men from Rushen in the south, small men from the white fuchsia-hidden farms of Ayre in the north, from forgotten holdings deep in the primeval forests of the Curraghs, from cottages in sycamore-shaded glens, from lonely houses on the sides of mountains, and from the narrow lanes of Peel that smell of wood-smoke and kippers, from the stately old capital of Castletown with its silver lime-stone castle, from the noble Welch Gothic range of King William's College, from Ramsey with its delicate Georgian Court House, from Douglas, that Naples of the North, from forgotten hamlets like Ronague on the slopes of South Barrule, from the stricken terraces by deserted lead-mines of Foxdale, from Laxey where the greatest water-wheel in the world stands idle for ever, and from the sheltered lanes of Port St. Mary, the Manxmen come to Tynwald fair. The little railway runs extra trains. All sorts of extraordinary rolling stock, made in the 'nineties and as good as ever, is drawn by little engines past creamy meadowsweet and brown mountain streams to the curious junction of St. John's. And there not far from the station is Tynwald Hill itself, an artificial mound of grass, eighty feet high with four circular terraces around it.

On July 5th, a cream canopy tops the mound to shelter the Governor of Man who will represent the King, and down the straight avenue that leads to the church white masts fly alternately the flags of Britain and of Man. St. John's Chapel is a golden granite spired building in that dashing and original style of romantic Gothic invented by John Welch which characterises almost all Manx established churches and which is Georgian in origin, though often Victorian in execution. The path to the church is strewn with rushes, offerings to a pagan sea god older than the Viking Tynwald mound. As eleven strikes, the sun streams down, a hymn from A. and M. is relayed from the church; the chief people in the island are assembled for public worship. The Coroners, the Captains of the Parishes, the Clergy in their robes, the Chairmen of the Town Commissioners of Peel, Ramsey and Castletown in frock coats, the Mayor of Douglas all in red and ermine; they step out into the sunlight from the west door. And so do the Vicar-General, the Archdeacon, the High Bailiff—all these legal-clerical-looking men—the Members of the House of Keys, their Chaplain and their Speaker, the Government Secretary, the Members of the Legislative Council, the Attorney-General, the two Deemsters in their robes of red who are the judges of the island, and the Lord Bishop of Sodor and Man—that luckless Bishop whose cathedral is a beautiful ruin of green slate and red sandstone on an islet overlooking Peel, that luckless Bishop who has a seat in the English House of Lords but no vote in it—who is second in command of the island. And now comes the Sword of State, a thirteenth-century Scandinavian relic, and behind it the Lieutenant-Governor himself with a posse of police and the Surgeon to the Household keeping up the rear. Slowly they ascend to Tynwald Hill, the Governor to the top and the rest in order of importance on terraces below. The Coroner fences the court. Then the Deemster reads out the latest laws in English and a priest reads them out again in Manx. It is all beautifully organised and it goes on for a long time. But here in this ancient circle of the hills time seems nothing. As the old Manx language is read out, the sun shines down on us, although the peaks of every mountain round us are hidden in clouds. It is always fine, I am told, at St. John's on Tynwald Day. The magician who lived in the island up to the fifth century used to make a mist to hide the island from its invaders, and it is certainly true that whenever Man has been visited by English king or queen it has been shrouded in mist, even at a recent visit of King George VI.

43

Fishing and farming were once the chief industries of the Manx. Fishing has dwindled so that there are now only nine boats Manx-manned and owned among all the little drifters that set out into the evening for herrings. The other hundred are mostly Scottish. And even farming takes second place to the greatest Manx industry, which is catering.

This brings me to the most enjoyable thing in all the enjoyment of Man—the visitors. I wish I knew when it was that these mass migrations from Lancashire started. Perhaps I can tell most easily from looking at Douglas. If I stand on Douglas Head and look across that noble sweep to Onchan Head, before the fairy lights are on and while the sun setting behind the mountains still lets me see the outline of the houses on the front, I can trace the recent history of the island.

The original Douglas at my feet, around the harbour, is a small fishing port, not half so beautiful as Castletown further down this eastern coast—Castletown with its magnificent medieval-moated and turreted castle, its box-pewed, three-deckered, still unspoilt church, its exciting stone police station by Baillie Scott, and its Doric column to Governor Smelt. What made Douglas grow was its natural scenery, but people did not notice natural scenery until Georgian times. The last Duke of Atholl to be governor had the Shrewsbury architect George Stewart design him, in 1804, a palace on this noble sweep of bay. It is known today in its smooth, silvery stone as Castle Mona Hotel. Its dining-room is the finest room on the island, the Adam style at its simplest and most graceful. Only that exquisite country house the Nunnery, in Walter Scott Gothic by John Pinch, compares with it. And after the Duke, the debtors escaping to Mona with some cash, and other visitors, built themselves romantic castles on these heights above the bay—Falcon Cliff, Fort Anne, Derby Castle. These are late Georgian castellated buildings designed to look like romantic ruins by John Welch who also built in 1832 the Tower of

44

Refuge on a rock in the middle of the water in Douglas Bay and so turned a looming danger into the semblance of an ancient castle. Then in the reign of William IV the gaps between the castles were filled in with stately stucco terraces, Brighton fashion (Windsor Terrace and Mount Pleasant are the best) sometimes high on the cliffs and here and there on the sea shore. The effect was and is magically beautiful. These Georgian terraces and Walter Scott, Peveril-of-the-Peak style castles flash out upon the cliff side. But this exclusive and romantic watering place cannot originally have been designed for half a million north-country folk—more likely for a few hundred half-pay officers eking out their pensions here where taxes are low.

I think the man of genius who turned the island into what it is, and saved it from ruin so that it is now financially prosperous, was Governor Loch. He improved the harbours and built the Loch Promenade in the 'sixties and 'seventies. Thereafter Douglas-style boarding-houses appeared in rows wherever there were gaps between the old terraces. They are innocent enough five-storeyed, bay-windowed, gabled buildings, gloomy behind, sea-gazing in front, rows and rows and rows of them so that the distant effect is of white paper folded into a concertina and perched here and there and everywhere along the shore. They are not as disfiguring as the modern bungalows and clumsily arranged electric light poles which ruin so much of the country part of Man. And now what with the T.T., the motor races, the improved harbours, the way everybody is out to be gay, *however* gloomy you are feeling you cannot be ill-humoured in Douglas. The boats arrive, the aeroplanes come down, young men and old in open shirts, sports coats and grey flannels, young girls and old in cheerful summer dresses, queue for ices, queue for shrimps, crowd round bars for glasses of delicious dry champagne, gaze from horse-trams over municipal flower beds to the Tower of Refuge and the sea, travel in luxury coaches round the island half asleep in one

45

another's arms till the sun sets behind the boarding-houses of Douglas and all the lights go up and the dance halls begin to fill. It is nine o'clock. There is still light in the sky. Father and mother, basking in one another's love, are sitting in chairs on the steps of the boarding-house; behind the front door peeps the inevitable castor oil plant in its china pot. Beside them sit the younger children, unnaturally good and quiet for fear they shall be sent up to bed while it is still light and while the moon rises huge and yellow above the purple bay. The elder children, grown up now, are off to the dance halls. Only a few rejected young men sit sadly on the steps among the ancients and the infants. The girls wear white dancing shoes and that is how you know whither they are bound. Two shillings or four-and-six, somewhere round that, is the cost of a ticket to dance. I like the Palace dance hall best. It has a parquet floor of sixteen thousand square feet and room for five thousand people. It is in a gay baroque style, cream and pink inside, and from the graceful roof hang Japanese lanterns out of a dangling forest of flags. A small and perfect dance band strikes up—ah, the dance bands of the Isle of Man! Soon a thousand couples are moving beautifully, the cotton dresses of the girls like vivid tulips in all this pale cream and pink, the sports coats and dark suits of the men a background to so much airy colour. The rhythmic dance is almost tribal, so that even a middle-aged spectator like me is caught up in mass excitement, pure and thrilling and profound.

And while the dance bands are playing in Douglas and the yellow moon is rising in its bay, on the western, wilder coast the herring fleet is setting out from Peel. The sun sets behind the rugged outline of the Castle and the ruined Cathedral and Round Tower enclosed within its walls. A stiffish west wind is blowing and the sea beyond the breakwater is dark green and choppy. The herring boats are disappearing into the sunset. Out of the harbour, round the castle island, the dying sun shines gold upon their polished sides. I stand alone upon a rock by Peel Castle. The smell of salt and wet earth is in my nostrils, the dark green slate of those old castle walls is at my side. Inland, the last rays of sun are lighting the winding lanes of Peel, the red sandstone of its church towers, and the soft protecting mountains behind it of the Isle of Man. Here, salt spray, seagulls, wild rocks and cavernous cliffs. Beyond those mountains the dance halls of Douglas and the dance-band leader in his faultless tails. An isle of contrasts! A miniature of all the Western world.

7   ANTIQUARIAN PREJUDICE[1]

I COME to you fresh from Evensong and with my outlook widened. Architecture has a wider meaning than that which is commonly given to it. For architecture means not a house, or a single building or a church, or Sir Herbert Baker, or the glass at Chartres, but your surroundings; not a town or a street, but our whole over-populated island. It is concerned with where we eat, work, sleep, play, congregate, escape. It is our background, alas, often too permanent.

Gradually, after years of enforced blindness, we are becoming aware of it again. When we wake up one morning and find the view from our windows shadowed by a colossal block of flats built to look like Hampton Court piled on top of itself several times; when we are perhaps driven to live in a flat where the central heating will not turn off, where the picture rail is at the wrong height, where the lift whines like a mosquito at irregular intervals during the night, where Bing Crosby croons across the dark well, where the door won't shut because the wood has warped, where there is no sun or too much sun, where the nearest station is twenty minutes' walk; when we go to a village we used to know and find it a town, and a muddled town at that; when we hear, as I heard the other day, of the bay window of a modern Tudor house lifted by a storm from its setting and flung over the opposite house-tops while the family in the parlour was at Sunday dinner; when we hear of another modern semi-detached villa where

[1] Originally delivered as a lecture (1937) to the Group Theatre and published as No. 3 of *Hogarth Sixpenny Pamphlets*.

the grate fell out of the chimney-breast and had to be screwed in again, and at spring-cleaning time the family next door found its piano screwed to the wall; when we see the squares of London being transformed into wells for blocks of flats—witness Berkeley Square; when we hear of Mr. Rudolf Palumbo putting up things which will scrape as much of the London sky as the L.C.C. will allow, in places which were left open by the foresight and civic sense of our forefathers; when we see super-cinemas made in the manner of Stockholm Town Hall, and town halls made in the manner of Wembley Exhibition; when we see every field and every hill striped with imitation Tudor or Queen Anne villas; when we learn that these are all owned through building societies, and realise that the luckless occupants will find themselves in a few years' time saddled with a slum; when we realise that each of these occupants is a landowner of potential slum property which nothing but a change of heart, to be wrought by nothing short of a miracle, will induce him to give up; when we hear of the party politics which hinder any constructive architectural effort of the L.C.C.; when we hear, learn, see all this and a great deal more which would cause this easily written diatribe to continue for the rest of this essay; when we hear all this, those of us with a sense of justice, let alone a love of good building, begin to think that there is something wrong with architecture today.   We begin to notice our surroundings.

It would be outside the scope of what I am saying to bring in all the causes of this muddle.   But one cause at least I can indicate, and can analyse, that of antiquarian prejudice.   A love of the ancient has bitten into most of us.   I suppose everyone who feels afraid, and most of us do, of the delightful benefits which science has bestowed on us, and everyone who feels a certain disgust, as most of us do, at the financial machinations of people behind the building trade, prefers looking back to looking at the present.   Certainly we err in not looking forward, largely because the immediate present makes us feel we dare not do so.

For myself, almost any age seems civilised except that in which I live. My preference is for the first quarter of the nineteenth century in England when the æsthetic outlook seems to have been particularly bright. The generation before mine preferred the reign of Queen Anne and mid-eighteenth-century work. A glance at fashionable antique shops will prove to you that that is the generation which still has the purchasing power. The generation before that preferred the Jacobean—witness Willett houses in Sloane Street district, Hampstead, and the grander suburbs of London; our grandfathers and colonials still have their furnishing schemes decided for them by certain big shops. The generation before that preferred the later medieval styles—witness the work of Bodley and Garner, Burne-Jones and William Morris. The generation before that preferred the thirteenth century—witness the spiky Gothic churches, spraying out of the stucco, the Albert Memorial, St. Mary Abbot's, Kensington, and the fine Catholic Apostolic in Gordon Square.

The generation before that—and we are back in that first quarter of the nineteenth century which I so greatly admire—hardly looked back at all, except in a literary way, building here a miniature Abbotsford, there a minor Fonthill, and in St. Pancras New Church, a perfect reproduction of various details of Greek Temples. The Gothic, Norman or Greek revivals of those days were essentially original and vigorous. They were not dead reproduction. They were a harmless veneer, covering interiors adapted to contemporary life. Alongside them grew up those early experiments in cast iron and glass which resulted in the Crystal Palace, almost the only flower of a new architecture which was able to thrust up its head among the hothouse revivals by which it was eventually choked. Alongside them, too, grew up the new architecture of railways, canals and planned building estates of which vestiges have been allowed to remain: King's Cross station; the Grand Junction canals; Kennington; the Regent's Park; the New River Company's property, to cite London alone. In fact, one may say that, until the 'forties and in certain instances until later, architecture had full confidence in itself.

It is not my intention to cover, as has been so often covered before, the history of the Gothic and other revivals during the nineteenth century. Instead, I will divide architecture into four groups, and show where antiquarianism has stepped in to hinder it; then I will show where the over-reaction or under-reaction from antiquarianism has done an equal amount of harm. The four groups are: Ecclesiastical, Monumental, Domestic and Planned.

There is much to say about antiquarianism in relation to ecclesiastical building, despite the fact that more churches seem to be pulled down than put up. Though it is not the authoritative opinion of the Church—*vide* the Seventh Report of the Central Council for the Care of Churches—it seems to be the æsthetic influence of bishops and lesser clergy that causes only eighteenth- and early nineteenth-century churches to be pulled down, and of them we have too few examples. But those who have visited episcopal palaces will know the cheerful chintzes, the Oxford frames, the electroliers, the islands of mat that one leaps to, like George Israel jumping the icefloes with the Moravian Gospel to Poland, on one's way from bed to the brass can of tepid water; you will know the taste in leatherwork of the Bishop's wife, the cork mats on the refectory table; you who know these— for what is an episcopal palace but the rectory spread thinly over a multitude of rooms?—you who know these, will not be surprised to hear that one Renaissance church has been demolished as "pagan," and that another has been scheduled for demolition. You who know how the homes of the spiritually minded are furnished, how much good nature and genuine humility there are in those homes, have probably become, with me, no longer surprised at the æsthetic arrogance of their inhabitants. Yet among no section of the public is such witting antiquarianism rampant as among the clergy and, more especially, their wives. And when we realise that the clergy, despite new legislation

51

in the matter of faculties, are able with one lick of vermilion or orange, one fretsaw saint, one furtive hatchet-stroke into box-pew, hatchment or commandment-board, to ruin the embodiment in stone and wood of generations of English church people—when we realise this, then indeed we will look apprehensively at the rectory drawing-room when we go to get the key of the church.   If the parish is poor and the rector, too, all is well, the church will not be harmed.   But if the walls of the rectory show signs of an interest in art; if plaster saints, woodcuts in the manner of Eric Gill, etchings, Brangwyns, Margaret W. Tarrants predominate over the more decent taste for family photographs and Arundel prints, then hey presto! before we know where we are there will be a box-pew cleared away to make a children's corner, a decent classic monument destroyed to reveal a conjectured wall-painting, a Royal Arms removed as "not devotional," and the church will be transformed into a little scrap album to contain bits and oddments from church-furnishers and artistic ladies' handicrafts shops wherever the name of an E.E. piscina is held in high esteem.

What, you may ask, has this to do with antiquarianism?   To which I reply that, like E.E. piscinæ, it has everything.   The clergy are medievalists almost to a man.   And not medievalists of a lovable kind.   Theirs is the mental calibre of Sir Gilbert Scott, translated into the present day.   They have not the originality of Butterfield, Burges, Teulon or Comper, in their play with Gothic.   Palgrave writing of the Albert Cross (Memorial) says: "It fails, not because much of it is inspired from older sources—for in all architecture copying holds a great place—but because it is *unimaginative* copying, and hence neither fused into harmony with itself, nor appropriate to its situation. Imagination is the vital quality in art; and the want of it will always be found to resolve itself into want of intelligence."   Comper has lent me his copy of Palgrave's book, and he has pencilled in the margin against this passage, "mostly true."   Palgrave's strictures and Comper's comment may be applied to the clergy and to antiquarians (or archæologists as they now call themselves) generally. Let us see, while we are dealing with these literal archæologists, and before we pass on to the wider influence of antiquarian prejudice, what their outlook is. The best illustration I can think of is to put side by side passages of prose, each describing the same place. It gives you an idea, incidentally, of the debasement of topographical literature. First: *The Guide*, 1901; reprinted 1902, '03, '04, '05, '06, '07, '08, '09, '10, '14, '18, '20, '21, '22, '23, '24, '25, '26, '27, '28, '29, etc.:

> "*Tickleby Tomcat*. (Station: West Lincolnshire Light Railway—1½ miles.)—The manor of Tuckoldbury is mentioned in Domesday Book as being worth XVIII pence, and held by one Lanfranc de Tuckoldbury, its glebes, messuages, and pottages for all time. Thence the manor of Tuckoldbury seems to have had that of Tommecutte added to it by bill of Attainder from Simon de Montfort. It passed from the family of the Lanfranc mentioned in Domesday to John Strongitharm, Abbot. We have no record of the goodly abbot's residence on the twin estates, though doubtless the revenues derived therefrom to the Abbey of Walsinghame, where a certain 'John String-i-ham' was abbot in 1301, and who can probably be identified with the John Strongitharm (see *Victoria County History*, Vol. I, p. 659). At the dissolution of the monasteries the estates passed to one Edward Stronghorn, doubtless a relative of our abbot, in whose family it remained until comparatively recent times (1682). Tomcat Park is modern.
>
> "The Church, Norm., E.E., Dec., with Perp. features; Trans. window in S. Transept, has an interesting double piscina in the N. Porch."

That's the stuff for tourists—also for the vicar who has had it copied out in script and hung framed above the alms box, an inducement, if ever there was one, to contribute to the fabric of a building which has so interesting a record in the annals of our land. Notice the grisly facetiousness of "one Lanfranc" and "the goodly abbot" and "a certain John String-i-ham."

The vicar's wife, however, is on the C.P.R.E., and by no means so dry-as-dust an antiquarian. She much prefers the account of the village given by Mr. Sussex Tankard in his popular work, *Hiking down the Valleys Wild,* based perhaps on *The Guide* and the Ordnance Map:

> First to the right after Claxby, then sharp left again down a winding lane, and another turn to the right at the fork, and you are in Tickleby Tomcat. There's something of a good old Lincolnshire ring about a name like Tickleby Tomcat, and, indeed, the name goes back in various forms till Domesday. Now there is something about picturesque Tickleby that makes it quite possible to imagine that Norman Barons and monks of old took (like Abbot Strongitharm, of whom more anon) pleasure in leaning over picturesque Tickleby Bridge—or perhaps there was only a ford then—watching the beautiful Tickold wind its way to the North Sea. The ancient church has a fine double piscina in the porch on the North side.

You will notice the plentiful scattering of the words "picturesque," "ancient," "fine," "beautiful"—adjectives taken straight from antiquarian literature and consequently now become quite meaningless. "Picturesque" may be used fearlessly to describe anything remote which one has not had time to visit; "Beautiful" is equally safe with a stream that is not actually a sewer, and directions of a most precise kind can be written by anyone able to read a map. "Ancient" is a pretty safe word for a country church which *Kelly's Directory* does not describe as having been rebuilt by Sir Gilbert Scott or Street, and "piscinæ," if they are distinguishable as piscinæ, are always "fine." So are aumbries, stoups, apses, lancets, squints, niches and other paraphernalia.

So far we have seen Tickleby Tomcat through the eyes of persons, who, for all we know, have never been there. True, the writer of *The Guide* may have visited the church to rub a brass, but finding no brass, have gone off in a temper as black as his own heel ball, pausing to note the piscina to which an antiquarian vicar desperately drew his attention.

What is Tickleby Tomcat really like? We shall never know. Let me point what it may well be. Fifty grey limestone cottages with thatched roofs in a clay district where oaks and elms are numerous. There are no hills near, and an east wind comes straight off the east coast twenty miles away, full of salt and very cold. The four most prominent features of the village are: (1) a sequence of Georgian bow-windowed shop-fronts in the main street; (2) a water tower in the Scottish Baronial style; (3) Tomcat Park, a decayed house, possibly early Georgian, inhabited by the surviving sister of an extinct and unimportant peer. In the Park are some temples, a grotto and an obelisk ascribed to Sir William Chambers. The house inside has complete Georgian fittings, oil-lamps, portraits, furniture, earth-closets, except in the new wing, which is 1880 Tudor, result of a final bust on the part of the late peer; (4) a line of fancy bungalows, connected with the sugar beet industry, along the road for half a mile towards Claxby. They were put up too recently to be marked on Mr. Sussex Tankard's map. The bridge, which he chats about so hopefully, is a concrete structure in the 1920 Municipal Renaissance style, put up by the Horncastle Rural District Council.

I say this having fallen into topographical traps of a like nature myself in the course of writing guide-books.

The church is the one building in the village of no interest at all. It was so generously restored by our peer that any of the Perp., E.E., etc., features remain in such a rebuilt state as to be almost new. The piscina was left out by the architect, Mr. G. E. Street[1]—and consequently left in the N. Porch It now consists of some pieces of decayed stone which may well have come off the vicarage rockery.

Apart from Tomcat Park, the only objects of interest (notice the phrase) are the people. But antiquarianism is not interested in people.

I fear that this disquisition from ecclesiastical matters to topographical writing may have caused you to lose the thread of what little argument there was before. Back again, then.

[1] I have now learned that Street was a severe but not merciless restorer and he was dead by 1881. One of the Fowlers of Louth is more likely to have "restored" a Lincolnshire church.

We have three more groups of architecture to consider in the green cathedral-glass light of antiquarian prejudice. Here the light is less direct, less obviously antiquarian, but none the less depressing.

By monumental architecture I mean public libraries, town halls, banks, swimming-baths, offices, railway stations. We have many fine examples of buildings in the monumental style from the past—Greenwich Hospital, Somerset House, St. George's Hall (Liverpool), Euston Hall and great Arch, the Houses of Parliament, King's Cross Station, each representing the best of the various phases of English secular architecture. Why is it that the twentieth century has produced not a single monumental English building of any real excellence? Why is it that Waterloo Station is a grandiose muddle of pre-war sculpture stuck on to an honest industrial building? What makes the new Regent Street such a grimy joke? Why is South Africa House so hideous? Why do we dread every steel scaffolding for what is going to be spread across it? First, there is the timidity miscalled "tradition," but really antiquarianism, which enslaves be-knighted architects. You are told that it is the Building Acts which cause every London building to be cloaked with Portland stone. This is not so, but even if it were so the Building Acts would not prescribe Corinthian columns and commercial Baroque to be sculpted on as well. "Tradition" has been aptly described by the late A. R. Powys as *digested experience*. Can it be, then, that all contemporary architects of English monumental work have been suffering from indigestion? Yes, it can. And it is as unpleasant for them as it is for us. All of them, except perhaps Sir Reginald Blomfield, must realise that their banks and libraries are somehow not quite like St. George's Hall, Greenwich Hospital, the Fitzwilliam, the Louvre, or whatever they intended them to be like—in spirit, of course, not in plan. I think the failure comes from "antiquarianism"; they think that columns and swags are "traditional"; really these appendages become antiques, unless they can be moulded into an individual style which none of the knighted architects—except now and then Sir Edwin Lutyens—has the genius to do. On the other hand, to go to the opposite extreme and let the new frightening materials, that they never knew when they were young men, do the job for them as Paxton let cast iron or glass do *his* job at the Crystal Palace, this savours of Bolshevism. For an antiquarian reason, to which the present state of architecture in U.S.S.R. gives the direct lie, an honest, plain structure of steel, glass, and/or reinforced concrete is considered Bolshevistic or international. And, of course, since the new materials have burst on the world more or less simultaneously, and since everyone who experiments with them is bound to produce work similar to that in a country hundreds of miles away, the style is bound to seem international. But no more and no less international than the graves of the Bronze Age men or the fortresses of the Middle Ages.

I must add here a parenthesis. Upholders of new methods of building are inclined, in their enthusiasm, to think that no further use can be made of the so-called traditional styles; that brick and stone, columns and swags are finished. As far as big office blocks and monumental secular architecture of any size are concerned, they are. St. George's Hall and the Houses of Parliament are final examples of the brick and stone architecture—and there is a good deal of cast iron in *them*. But these buildings are satisfactory because they are built out of materials to which this decoration, whether structural or not, was suited, and because they were built by men of genius capable of moulding a style of their own.

We all know the antiquarianism that besets the third group, domestic architecture. So well do we know it that it is hardly worth while trotting out the old jokes. Walk, some sunny afternoon as I have done, through any post-war suburb—and almost any place you visit in England *is* a post-war suburb. Look up, while the perambulator creaks beside you and the children skip over the squares of paving to the too-distant park, look up at the quiet houses that flank the interminable avenue. In poorer districts only a variation in the stained glass of a front door, the juxtaposition of gable beams, or greater or less repulsiveness in the texture of rough-cast differentiates one house from another. In twenty years' time, when the building societies have got more than their money back, only the standard roses dwarfing the Cotswold sundial, the flower-beds lovingly filled with tested seeds, will improve the appearance of the road. Bay windows will be falling out, foundations crumbling, plumbing leaking, leaded lights letting in the rain, the larder will be sheltered by the hood of that long-disused pram—the Happy Homestead to which Hubby smilingly gave Wifie the key, that little corner of a loving heart that is for ever Metroland, will be rather unpleasant. The L.P.T.B. will not bother to display its best posters on the underground station; the buses will be less frequent, the walk longer, the houses draughtier than ever.

In the richer districts Queen Anne vies with Tudor, as in St. John's Wood where some of the most arrogant, staring, badly-planned travesties of Queen Anne architecture flare up in place of the decent Early Victorian stucco which once made that district a sun-reflecting half-village among laburnums and pollarded limes. I think of two couplets from Longfellow's "Lady Wentworth," describing the dream-mansion of American riches, they describe the dream-mansion of England today:

> "*It was a pleasant mansion, an abode*
> *Near and yet hidden from the great high road,*
> *Sequestered among trees, a noble pile,*
> Baronial and Colonial in its style."

If ever antiquarianism disguising itself as "tradition" has affected the English landscape, it has affected it in domestic building. Though willing to be crushed in an argument on the subject, I am ready to admit that in certain villages of limestone, chalk or brick, the old methods of building are the right ones. The pitched roof, a

harmonious building material, even leaded lights (though not diamond panes) are permissible. But for our suburbs, that is to say for
the bulk of our population, it can only be a form of bogus traditionalism
backed by certain sinister influences in the building trade which has
permitted the present system to continue. Building can only be
carried on in fine weather. The houses once built, however badly,
cannot be removed except at very great expense. When the focus of
the population shifts, many London suburbs will be deserted and
terrifying like the pit villages of the north, from which much of
London's new population has come. They will be useless as agricultural lands, and hardly a worthy memorial of our so-called civilisation
to yet more archæologists in the future.

Every day one sees in the papers advertisements of portable houses.
Hideous indeed they often are. But that is the fault of architects.
Architects have been too wrapped up in "style," in bricks and foundations and whatnot, to devote their attention to the only solution of the
housing problem—the production of decent and convenient mass-
produced houses. These houses should be pre-fabricated, as was the
Crystal Palace, they should be and could be as well planned, as sound
and weather-proof as the best brick-built house. Pre-fabrication
would make it possible to remove these houses from one place to
another when they were wanted, and the land they had occupied
could go back to agriculture. Experiments in houses of this sort have
been made successfully in Germany and America. I see no hope for
the majority until they are made here. Lord Nuffield had a wonderful
opportunity to make them at his pressed-steel works at Oxford. He
missed it, and many of his workers are housed in some of the worst
speculative estates to be seen. Perhaps I am reading too much into
antiquarianism to attach it to such inertia as this.

Lastly comes planning, and with this I am too, perhaps, stretching
a point by laying the stress on antiquarianism. But planning (though
it comes last in this essay, it is the most important) is riddled with

various schools of thought. Schools of thought? First comes the School of No Thought. The L.C.C. pulled down Waterloo Bridge for reasons which it would be libellous to go into. Were they planning a great road north and south, quite straight? If so, why? Does the L.C.C. realise that motor cars do not mind going out of their way to avoid traffic halts? That circular roads would be cheaper and more practical? That horse traffic, to which the shortest route was the quickest, is now almost defunct?

Another example of the School of No Thought is that which puts up hefty blocks of flats, of the wrong height, in places where, for all we know, flats will not be wanted in ten years' time—the School of No Thought, which builds before it plans, is found in every English local authority. Only someone with the myopic eyesight of an antiquarian would put up houses and clear others away before some concerted scheme of planning, traffic, railways, was made. As it is, the estates are built, and transport at great expense and to the confusion of everything else comes lumbering along afterwards.

Perhaps it is antiquarianism, too, which dreams of England as a series of self-supporting garden suburbs surrounded by green belts. These antiquarians would have to go to Northumberland and Durham, the Welsh mountains or the distant "shires" before they could find a belt of any desirable width which could be called really green—any beyond that of leather which girdles up their own homespuns.

Finally, my mind switches to the last fruit of the excessive antiquarianism to which we are subject—the educated reaction from it, which results in "jazz-modern."

"Jazz-modern" is the product of insensitive minds. It is the decoration of art-school students. You all know it. The "modernistic suites" to be seen in hire-purchase catalogues, the dashing milk-bars which have dispensed with the need for capital letters. The monogram and new buildings of the G.W.R. at Paddington. In the 1920's jazz-modernism consisted of cubes, triangles and arrows in "poster colours"; everything from the frosted glass above the windows of a shop to the cushion in a punt was in this emancipated jazz manner. Perhaps even the arrogant modern designers who dared to think they could create mouldings and motifs, which it has taken centuries to evolve, perhaps even they grew afraid. Anyhow, the neo-Swedish style succeeded in favour. Little squashed flowers were engraved on glass (the new R.I.B.A. building is the cathedral of such decoration) or painted in ever-so-dainty shades of pastel pink and pastel green on to unstained birchwood. Later a style that was neither the one nor the other, but called "not too modern and not too traditional" was used, as it is now, for cinemas, churches and public buildings. Sir Giles Gilbert Scott is its most successful exponent. His library at Cambridge is only excelled by his new Bodleian as a "safe blending of tradition with modernism," whatever that may mean. In London the supreme example of the restrained jazz is his work at Battersea Power Station. There the good, tall chimneys were not allowed to smoke for themselves, an architect was called in to design some fluting part of the way up them. Give me Lot's Road. But Sir Giles has his great moments.

The reaction from antiquarianism has been almost as harmful as antiquarianism itself.

Before I finish, I would like to enquire into the causes of this extraordinary state.

There are the champions of antiquity. First the experts.

We know the expert by sight and by conversation. "Yes, very interesting, no doubt, but I'm afraid it's not in my period—you should see Popplethwaite. I believe he has done some work on the subject." Experts are short-sighted, probably from studying details for so long, they live in museums, they are a little scurfy, a little dirty, very precise and very damning of every other expert. They have that wonderful gift of turning life to death, interest to ashes. The only vitality visible in them is the heartiness of their contempt for the enquiring layman. Then they flower, then they love to dazzle him with words and with references. And that enquiring layman, who might be you or I, is sent home abashed. Perhaps he came to know about aquatints, having admired the colour-prints of Rowlandson and Malton. Admiration for his subject is not what the expert wants. Admiration for his knowledge is what he expects. Perhaps long ago the expert really did like aquatints, but now he only likes knowing about first proofs, raw state, etc., etc. His word for "beautiful" has become "important." He is as removed from the original purpose of his subject, be it aquatints for illustration, stained glass for telling a story, textile for decoration, as the mathematician from simple arithmetic.

Experts can live in museums and can be divorced entirely from the setting. Museums and the experts who run them are one of the penalties of antiquarianism. Not all museums, for there can obviously be such a thing as an inspiring museum—the picture galleries and sculpture halls. But whenever I walk through long galleries of spears and arrow-heads, of urns and sarcophagi, I do *not* feel myself taken back to the ancient civilisations. Rather I find myself admiring dignified architecture and thinking what a long walk it is from one end of the Museum to another, and how singularly lifeless the loveliest things appear as soon as they are in a little glass case with a label underneath them. Museums of the uninspired sort, and that is to say most museums, from Forest Hill to Bethnal Green, are the direct children of antiquarianism. They are places where you cannot see the woad for the spears, more often you cannot even see the spears, so remote, so distinct, so classified and subclassified are the little prongs of objects displayed. There is only one London museum of an antiquarian sort which really moves me, and that is Sir John Soane's, in Lincoln's Inn Fields. And this is interesting not only because of its wonderful plan and exquisite furniture and pictures, but also because it was Sir John's private house.

And along with museums and experts comes the research worker and his institute. Research is the curse of our age. "Research" is

the first step on the way to expertdom. There is so much research
going on nowadays that teachers are becoming scarce. Already in
the universities complaints are being made about there being too
many research students and research fellowships. And what, you
may ask, is all this research for? Goodness knows. There are at
Oxford students researching into modern languages. What are they
researching? Are they just being paid money to read minor authors
in the original? It looks like it. Research into art is useful, but
there can be and is too much of it. Every research student in art
means one less work of art—for it means the glorification of antiques
and the established, and less encouragement to the struggling artist. If
the tremendous amount of money that has been lavished on founding
the Courtauld Institute—an institute for breeding art critics and
antique dealers of the more expensive sort—had instead been given as
a fund for the encouragement and support of living artists, those among
my readers who are creative workers would be able to have the more
chance of earning a livelihood by what they like best. It is symptomatic of this age of antiquarianism that a thing like the Courtauld
Institute exists.

Next comes the authoritative attitude given to antiquarian research.
Allow me to quote from a recent review of a publication of the Royal
Commission on Historical Monuments:

> Why does the survey stop at 1714? I have tried to find some signifi-
> cance for the date. Queen Anne died, the Peace of Utrecht had been
> signed the year before, the South Sea Bubble had not yet burst. Why
> not 1814? or 1914? Why any date at all? Should not all buildings of
> merit have been included and rather fewer fragmentary moats and
> fifteenth-century fonts? Or did none of the Commissioners feel himself
> capable of deciding what constituted architectural merit? The F.S.A.'s
> have it, as usual.
>
> It is hard to treat a survey as complete which thus describes Syon
> House, containing Robert Adam's best interior work, "A large Tudor
> house, much altered in the eighteenth century, and incorporating an
> undercroft of the nunnery of Henry V." On a plan of Syon, the Adam

part is marked as "modern and uncertain." Strawberry Hill interests the Commissioners because some original chamfered ceiling beams are exposed. The only part of Osterley recommended for preservation is the Elizabethan stables. Needless to add, four badly-preserved earthworks, eleven churches (but not Little Stanmore with its early eighteenth-century painted walls, Handel's organ and the Chandos tomb, as these are a year or more later than 1714 and therefore "modern"), and several seventeenth-century houses are recommended as "specially worthy of preservation."

Town planning schemes, large Georgian and Regency houses in gardens, eighteenth- and nineteenth-century churches, the few surviving parks with their grottoes and temples, are considerations beneath the notice of the Royal Commissioners or, as they would term it, "outside their scope."

This survey is not only absurdly inadequate, it is also definitely harmful. It has all the authority of His Majesty's Stationery Office, and the well-sounding names of the Royal Commissioners behind it; it is sold at so low a price that one can only conclude that the work has been subsidised: it is just the sort of book that will be used as a Bible. Arrogant and ignorant county councillors and avaricious builders will use it as an excuse for pulling down more and more worthy architecture: "Uxbridge Town Hall, Mr. Chairman, is not mentioned in the Historical Monuments Book. It has therefore no historical interest or architectural merits." "Very well, Mr. Tudor Beam, we will make an order for demolition." [1]

After all this, imagine the position of the modern architect. Picture the young fellow to be put into a "profession" because trade is considered beneath him (another antiquarian prejudice). The young fellow hasn't exactly got a legal mind, like father; he's not much good at essays, so he can't write; he faints at the sight of blood, so he can't be a doctor. What is there for him to do? Architecture, of course. Architecture has registered itself as a profession. Unlike Art, Architecture is practical and respectable. Why, I know architects who, as they're good at business, go far, just like ordinary men. Where shall we send the fellow? To an architectural school of course, where he'll

[1] This state of things is now altered. Salaried antiquarians on behalf of the Ministry of Town and Country Planning now schedule some Georgian work.

meet a lot of other healthy-minded youngsters and learn to turn out prize-medal drawings to be judged by Mr. Maufe, and learn to make letters in all the latest type-faces, and elevations in all the latest mannerisms, and to cast simply lovely shadows down his elevations.

Are you surprised that with such people as this, frightened on the one side by the "dry-as-dust" antiquarian, tickled to death on the other by all the jolly tricks of a rebellious *moderne*, futuristic, Swedish, cubistic, yet tasteful nature—are you surprised that architecture in England is what it is? With an Ealing veneer of antiquity or *moderne*-ity.

The time-honoured system of apprenticeship and practical experience, of being articled to an architect who either repulses you so much you react against him as Bodley did to the elder Gilbert Scott, or evolve from him out of admiration as Soane did from the younger Dance—that system is over. That system created individualists, great men of whom Comper, Voysey, Ashbee, Lutyens, Baillie Scott and a few others survive.[1]

A man must be a great man, or a movement must be a disinterested one, to be able to ignore the noise of antiquarian prejudice shouting at its bastard, jazz-modernism. Down every street the bawling goes, from Selfridge's to Lilley & Skinner's, from Drage's to Waring & Gillows, from Ouitoo to Grosvenor Court; the roads slide with motor cars, the chasms are blue with petrol fumes, the sky roars with aeroplanes, deadly insects whose drone is like a dentist's drill in the brain; the pavements belch with the noise of radio shops, the public passages are too narrow, the public faces too pinched, the public food too inedible, the public mind too frightened; a ticket for this, a form for that, a set opinion about this, a standard dream of the unattainable. No wonder we lose our heads, no wonder we escape into the past. No wonder the old men are antiquarians and the mediocre diddled. I hope

[1] Comper alone survives (1951).

I have shown how antiquarian prejudice has something, but not all, to do with it. Greed and Careerism have much more. What will give us time to think? What will give us an opportunity to act? A Ministry of Fine Arts? A change of government? or a change of heart?

8 THE ARCHITECTURE OF ENTERTAINMENT

I F there is one word which can safely be applied to the constructions for entertainment it is the adjective *impermanent.* Fire consumes and fashion changes, new and more hideous structures arise on the sites of older and less hideous, as we continue to slide into deeper depths of barbarism. One day, no doubt, something more blatant than the tower of the Odeon Cinema in Leicester Square will challenge comparison with the steeple of St. Martin's-in-the-Fields. For the present we must gaze at the pseudo-functional monument of the serious 'thirties, watching it grow more and more dated every week, while the steeple of St. Martin's glows in its white Portland stone perfection, a dateless memorial of more settled days.

The architecture of entertainment, of fairs, exhibitions, concert halls and theatres may be considered alongside church building. Like churches, places of entertainment are where people go for short spells only—all except for the cleaners and permanent staff who may be compared to the nuns and priests of churches, and very heartily they may laugh at the comparison. But the difference is that while churches are built to last, places of entertainment are not.

Nothing is more empty than a deserted fairground. A walk through the White City with no one about, the baroque sculpture collapsing, the plaster façades damp-stained, the halls echoing and dusty, the railway lines for special trains which carried long-dead merry-makers, rusty and grass-grown, is macabre even in broad daylight. And empty race-courses seem emptier than that. But an

67

empty church is full, especially one in which the Consecrated Host is reserved in tabernacle or cupboard in the wall, with a light before it. Such a building may be alarming. One may feel oneself elbowed out by angels, but the emptiness is awe-inspiring, not desolate.

For the truth is that in England and Scotland and Wales fairs and entertainments are the cast-offs of the church. Their ancestors were hurled out of churches when the religious plays acted in naves were considered too secular. They waltzed away into the churchyard and then into a field near the church. And on the date of the patronal feast of the church, in many an English village today, a fair is held in a neighbouring field. When I look at the roundabouts and swings and hoop-la canopies gaily coloured in King's Lynn, in the same style as barges are coloured at Stoke Bruerne, and as some old-fashioned waggons are still painted, when I see these traditional colours of red and blue and gold and green twisting round the flashing mirrors which hide the steam organ, when I catch sight of flares or electric bulbs reflected in barley sugar rods of polished brass, I think how near the church these really are. I remember they must be derived from canopies over images carried with a mixture of reverence and guffaws, centuries ago in English sunlight. And I wish that this people's art would come back to churches: a little more vulgarity of painted wood, a little less of the church furnisher and the art-expert and a little more of the fair ground. For this colour decoration of old-fashioned fairs is the oldest and most permanent feature of the architecture of entertainment.

English visitors are often shocked by the garishness of patronal feasts and processions in the towns and villages of Italy and Spain. There, fair and church, entertainment and worship are undivorced. We are shocked because we have still such a Puritan sense of sin about pleasure that we drive it out into the open fields of the world. From these outcast fairs, from strolling players and booths and competitions grew up the entertainment business whose structures are the subject of this article.

Churches are built on reality, in the mystical sense of that word. Fairs, exhibitions, theatres and cinemas are built for daydreams of personal wish-fulfilment, which is a phrase for pride. No wonder then that, unlike churches, impermanence pervades them.

Architecturally, the most impermanent, the most quickly dated of entertainment buildings are exhibitions and cinemas. The first great exhibition of 1851 was undoubtedly beautiful within its limits. I have a peep-show perspective of it. Under a bright light the eye looks down long glass avenues (whose cast-iron columns were originally painted with bright reds and blues under the direction of Mr. Owen Jones, who later designed the pleasant colours of Paddington Station which have now been obliterated by cream paint). The eye is stayed by crystal fountains, statues and hangings, flags of all nations, the great elm trees of Hyde Park which the palace enclosed, ormolu lamps tandards and hundreds of ladies walking about in coloured crinolines. All seem bathed in sunlight. One does really, in this Victorian perspective, recapture the idea current at the time that everything was getting better and better and that this exhibition of the products of Industrial Art was the beginning of a material millenium of peace on earth and good will towards men. But Ruskin, who saw through most things, was suspicious. "We used to have a fair in our neighbourhood—a very fine one we thought it," he writes in *Ethics of The Dust*. "You never saw such an one; but if you look at the engraving of Turner's 'St. Catherine's Hill' you will see what it was like. There were curious booths, carried on poles; and peep-shows; and music, with plenty of drums and cymbals; and much barley sugar and ginger-bread and the like; and in the alleys of this fair the London populace would enjoy themselves, after their fashion, very thoroughly. Well, the little Pthah set to work on it one day; he made the wooden poles into iron ones, and put them across, like his own crooked legs, so that you always fall over them if you don't look where you are going; and he turned all the canvas into panes of glass, and put it up on his iron cross-poles; and made all the little booths into one great booth;—and people said it was very fine, and a new style of architecture and Mr. Dickens said nothing was ever like it in Fairyland, which was very true." And he then proceeds to pour scorn on the exhibits. The Crystal Palace was indeed a new style of architecture. It was the first prefab, brought in numbered pieces in carts from the factories and erected swiftly in a public park. There is something ironic in the way this impermanent architecture, so well suited to an exhibition of lifeless industrial products, should have been resurrected in this century to make buildings which of all should be most permanent—homes for families.

The impermanent, utilitarian style of the Crystal Palace was, despite Ruskin's strictures, just the thing if industrial exhibitions were to continue. Yet later exhibitions, Alexandra Palace (1873), Olympia (1886), Earls Court (1912), The White City (1913), Wembley (1924), to cite London alone, seem to have been inspired by an over-confidence in material success. They are permanent buildings without that flimsy semi-rurality which must have been the charm of Pleasure Gardens like Vauxhall, Cremorne and Rosherville. Not that I would condemn them. All lovers of the useless, and they must be increasing in Britain hourly, could hardly fail to delight in the Alexandra Palace before the war. What a pleasure it was to tread acres of echoing boards past disused slot machines in search of the roller-skating rink where the huge steam organ would be playing to a few swirling couples, what a pleasure to open a wrong door, as I once did, to find Gracie Fields with a full chorus behind her, singing to an empty theatre. Gas, brickwork, silent dark towers, wet and windy amusement parks, bandstands where no silver band has played for twenty years, all these are associated with deserted exhibitions—and what terrible crimes, hinted at by Denton Welch or invented by Graham Greene, may not be perpetrated in the dark, deserted refreshment rooms or cloak-rooms where water drips everlastingly into stained, cracked and no longer hygienic porcelain. All that is part of the romance of decay.

As soon as exhibitions become permanent buildings like those I have mentioned, they quickly look out-of-date Their appeal is in being in the very latest style when they are erected.   Decoration, to convey the latest style, even if it is a coating of chromium pseudo-simplicity as at the Glasgow Exhibition of the nineteen-thirties, must predominate.   Hence the sad wildernesses of the White City, hence that mysterious area of minor Metroland around the Wembley Stadium where for all I know those concrete temples of Empire may still be standing among thin poplars and railway lines.

Cinemas too have their origin in fairs. They were, in living memory, booths where people paid a few pence to see the phenomenon of moving photographs. The exaggerated language of the huckster, "the most daring, stupendous, thrilling spectacle ever staged in the history of the universe," applies as much to the architecture of the cinema as it does to the language of the playbills, trailers and advertisements of films in the daily prints.   However much the film, so far as producers and directors are concerned, may progress towards an art, the exhibition side is still in the hands of those who have the mentality of the old fairs.   There is hardly a cinema in Britain, except for a highbrow exception like The Curzon, which is not architecturally on the outside a showy attempt to be up-to-date.   The interiors, whether "atmospheric" and designed to look like the Garden of Allah, a Moorish mosque or Imperial Rome, are designed as an exotic day-dream.   That day-dream looks particularly pitiful in daylight when the manager has not yet assumed his boiled shirt.   The earliest cinemas to be erected as permanent buildings may still be seen in some suburban and provincial high roads, the words ELECTRIC PALACE done in plaster among baroque twirls reminiscent of the White City, and a little pay box in mahogany protruding out below the colossal entrance arch.   They are survivals of the days when the cinema needed to attract people to go in.   There is no need for a flashy entrance now, for the cinemas are the chapels of most of our people who feel it a sin not to attend each change of programme.   The chief problem is to hold their increasingly sophisticated attention once they are inside. Slap up-to-date decoration may have something to do with that. There seems to me more sense in the comparatively modest façades of the Granada cinemas whose wildly fantastic interior decoration may possibly be changed as different styles come in, to suit another popular mood.

Music-halls come half-way between the cinemas and the theatre. Their origin is older and they are more homely.   They started as entertainments in public-houses and they ended as theatres with this single difference, that the bar opened straight into the auditorium as at dear old Collins's on Islington Green.

Theatres themselves are an older and more respectable form of architecture, Renaissance in origin—it would be absurd to connect them with the theatres of Ancient Greece and Rome since, in this country at any rate, theatres did not exist until after the Reformation. Nor do many of the older ones survive.   The round and open wooden theatres of Shakespeare's time, Wren's Drury Lane, the magic effects created by de Loutherbourg with real waterfalls at Sadler's Wells, not all the water in the New River has saved.   They were destroyed by either fire or fashion.   The most complete survival is the Theatre Royal at Bristol and even that is largely 1800 in date.   Mr. John Summerson, that learned and mordantly entertaining writer on architecture, says that very little of their history is known.   "The theatres of this country have never been much studied as architecture, though many books have been written on their owners, lessees and managers and the men and women whom their audiences have applauded."   And this is surprising, for when great dramatists were alive and actors like Garrick, whom all the world of intellect knew, the best architects were found to design theatres.   James Wyatt and

Henry Holland both built Drury Lane theatres, Nash designed the Haymarket, Smirke Covent Garden, Foulston designed Plymouth's Theatre Royal. All these buildings have been destroyed or altered out of recognition "by successive generations of profit-eager lessees."

Many fine Victorian theatres survive of which the best is the Theatre Royal at Newcastle (Benjamin Green, architect), almost a Georgian building and mercifully preserved from successive generations of fashion. In London the noblest surviving building—in my opinion more impressive within and without than Covent Garden—is the Royal English Opera House (1892, Thomas Collcutt, architect), now called the Palace Theatre. This is on an irregularly shaped island site. Its main façade on Cambridge Circus is concave and the awkwardness of the corners of such a façade is overcome by graceful octagonal turrets. The dressing rooms are all along the Shaftesbury Avenue side of the building and serve as a buffer against the noise of that main thoroughfare. The building slopes inwards from the auditorium and is acoustically a great success, though it is built on the opposite principles to those generally employed in theatre design. The three tiers of galleries are cantilevered out—a revolution at the time—so that no columns obstruct the view of the audience. The decoration throughout is scholarly Flemish Renaissance. Nothing is skimped and the entrance hall and staircases are rich in those contrasting marbles Collcutt delighted to use and which he employed so effectively in the Holborn Restaurant. The Palace is the only theatre architecture of the last sixty years in London, or for that matter the provinces, which climbs into the regions of a work of art. But many have a splendid richness as those by Charles John Phipps (1835–97), notably His Majesty's which was completed in the year of his death. Phipps designed some graceful, exuberant provincial theatres, of which The Gaiety, Dublin, is a still unspoiled example.

Many of London's smaller theatres preserved a charming quality of an Edwardian or late Victorian drawing room, with their whitewood or mahogany, plush seats and watered silk panels and electroliers. In the cheaper parts of these houses were the Dickensian fishtail gas-lights in wire cages in long stone staircases and passages. But these little theatres of which the Criterion and the Comedy were out-standing examples, have been stippled, pickled, shaved, sprayed, chromiumed or simplified according to D.I.A. rules of good taste so as to have lost most of their character. Only the St. James's survives as a charming period piece.

Fire is, until the next war, better controlled than before. The enemy of old-fashioned theatres today is fashion. Fashion has about it that impermanence which suits the impermanent architecture of entertainment. But if ever a man wants to study a popular style exaggerated to its vulgarest terms, let him look at the decoration of the buildings of entertainment. Cherubs will have chubbier cheeks and bottoms, caryatids have more protuberant breasts, *art nouveau* water lilies be more attenuated, cubes and triangles outstrip the ugliest followers of the worst of Picasso's cubist period, and if the word goes round "be functional" wall spaces will be plainer, chromium shinier, off-white be more off-white in or upon the theatres, cinemas, music halls, exhibition buildings, bandstands, piers and restaurants of the kingdom. Only the fairs survive.

9 LONDON RAILWAY STATIONS

THE study of railway stations is something like the study of churches. It can be turned into archæological detection work. For piscina, read cast-iron lamp bracket; for arcading, read girder construction; for transepts, read waiting-rooms; for hangings, read tin advertisements. Then with very little practice anyone with an eye for detail can date the objects inspected.

Picture a disused platform of a rather forgotten station, let us say South Hampstead, the first station after Euston ($2\frac{1}{2}$ miles) on the old L.M.S. electric line to Watford. It opens late and shuts early and few people seem to use it. When I was a boy we called it Loudon Road and the booking office building stood, as it still stands, looking rather like a small mid-Victorian brick Vicarage, harmonising happily with the Gothic fancies of this lilac-shaded part of St. John's Wood. I should think from the style of architecture it was built in the late 'seventies by which time enough platforms had been constructed at Euston to make it possible for the London & North Western to run an enlarged suburban service. I have never departed from nor alighted at South Hampstead. Not being modern, my hours are too long either side of the day to take advantage of its times of opening. I prefer to imagine the station. I like to think that it contains the various fittings of a former age for which my eye is always on the watch when I use an unfamiliar station. Perhaps there are some very old tickets in the booking office—a first-class return to Chalk Farm (which would mean going down to Euston and coming back again), would

probably be printed with "Loudon Road" and the letters L.N.W.R.
Under the treads of the stairs to the platform there may be those tin
advertisements saying IRON JELLOIDS, IRON JELLOIDS, IRON
JELLOIDS in blue on an orange ground, insisting, as one ascends, on
the weakness of one's heart and its need for the stamina which those
pills supply. Still in imagination, I walk right down to the end of the
platform to the oldest lamp standard, a graceful thing on twisted
columns with, perhaps, a six-sided glass cage for the gas-burner and
the name of the iron foundry where it was made at the base of its
column. Against the station wall there may be tin signs for MAZA-
WATTEE TEA and the still-familiar black and blue splodge of
STEPHEN'S INK on a white ground. And, of course, there will be
those two old friends VENO'S LIGHTNING COUGH CURE and
DR. J. COLLIS BROWNE'S CHLORODYNE.

Then what waiting rooms may there not be! Gothic Revival
cast-iron grates in which no fire has been lighted since the days when
a mountain of glowing coal warmed the early-morning pin-striped
bottoms of city gentlemen who used this station as the preliminary
part of a journey from Boundary Road to Euston, thence by steam
train on the inner circle from Euston Square to Aldersgate. (Ah,
Aldersgate! alas the Refreshment Room has been bombed, the
Refreshment Room at the top of the steps surveying all four platforms from the height of the great semi-circular glass roof, that Refreshment room where, as Mr. John Hayward once pointed out to me, the
words AFTERNOON TEAS A SPECIALITY were affixed in letters
of white china to the plate-glass window). The walls of the waiting
room will be green. The lighting gas. There will be perhaps be a
framed collection of photographs, "Beauty spots" of the L. & N.W.R.
—Killarney; Sackville Street, Dublin; Blarney Castle (the L. &
N.W. always liked to give the impression that it owned all the Irish
railways); George's Landing Stage, Liverpool; Bettws-y-coed;
Warwick Castle. These will be in sepia with gilt lettering on the

wooden surround. Then there will be a framed looking-glass in which it will be impossible to see all one's face at once because painted on the surface are the words IDRIS TABLE WATERS and a long maiden in clothes rather like a water lily holding in her hand a sparkling glass of IDRIS. These are but some of the delights I imagine there may be at South Hampstead.

The serious scholar of London railway stations will make the historical approach. I unfold the map of my *Bradshaw's Railway Companion for* 1841. London shrinks to its size a hundred and nine years ago. I notice that there were fields beyond Regent's Park and Pentonville and Islington and Hackney. Bethnal Green was in London, Stratford was not. South-east of Bermondsey and south of Walworth there were still fields between terraces and squares, fields that in two years were to be filled with either Italianate merchants' houses amid laurel shrubbery or with rows of two-storey artisans' dwellings. Chelsea and Brompton and Kensington still had separate personalities. No railways dared to invade the centre of London. Westminster was even more sacred than the City. There they are on the map, little pink lines, pushing tentatively towards the heart of the metropolis.

These early stations, you must remember, are part of the Georgian age. They are stately but not sumptuous. They are spreading but not soaring. They suggest coaches pulled by iron horses. They are merely another sort of posting inn, not something private, railed off and of another world, which railways have now become. They are the stables of the iron horses and they blend naturally with the drays which clatter over cobbles towards them and the carriages which are unloaded from them and pulled away by horses to the noblemen's houses of Mayfair. Euston (1837), London Bridge (1838), Paddington (1839) are still on their original sites. Philip Hardwick's magnificent Doric Arch of granite (1837) at Euston originally had two lodges flanking each side and was visible from the Euston road; the outer pairs of these have been destroyed. It was the gateway not only to all the country houses of the North, but also to a new age. The little iron sheds of the station behind it, so ridiculed by Pugin, are rather an anti-climax. Successive generations have treated this noble arch scurvily and its glory has been hidden by the Euston Hotel. As an essay of the Greek Revival, I consider the arch even now, almost shorn of its lodges, the noblest thing in London, nobler even than St. Pancras church or the British Museum or the Hyde Park Screen. Only one building rivalled it and that was Rennie's Waterloo Bridge. The L.M.S. made determined efforts to remove Euston Arch altogether. British Railways will probably succeed in doing so, for no one, except you and me, dear reader, yet believes that there can be anything beautiful about a railway station.

London Bridge, now a shattered collection of girders and temporary-looking platforms, has little to show of the old terminus of the Greenwich Railway, that remarkable line carried on 878 brick arches, which was merged with the South-Eastern and Chatham. There is a spacious dignity, created by white brick walls and an arching roof, about the Terminus part of the station whence trains depart over a loop line via the Crystal Palace (Low Level) and Norwood to Victoria, through Italianate stations and brick cuttings and sudden elevations from which one may see the brick Italianate houses of Ruskin's South London, the prehistoric monsters of the Crystal Palace Park and perhaps glimpse Sherlock Holmes hiding amid the laurels, lamp posts and ivy-clad clinker of a merchant's private drive.

The severe nine-arched entrance of Paddington has disappeared entirely, though the space in front of where it stood, now under glass, is still known as "the lawn." But two others of these six early stations survive. Nine Elms, erected in 1838 by Sir William Tite (architect of the Royal Exchange) as the terminus of the South Western Railway, may be found standing, classic, stuccoed and deserted, amid the gas-works, goods yards and factories of that district where strikes seem often to originate. There are no passengers and the more important goods yards seem to be in another part of Nine Elms, so that this building and its platforms are an early station survival. I know of no more complete example except Philip Hardwick's Great arch at the old and disused terminus in Birmingham of the London to Birmingham Railway.

A smaller London station of this period is now out of reach of the public. It is the Blackwall terminus of the old London and Blackwall Railway. Those frequent and quite empty trains of the Blackwall Railway ran from a special platform of Fenchurch Street. I remember them well. Like stage-coaches they rumbled slowly past East-End chimney pots, wharves and shipping, stopping at black and empty stations, till they came to a final halt at Blackwall station, a handsome building in white brick and Portland stone, from an Italianate design by Sir William Tite. When one emerged there was nothing to see beyond it but a cobbled quay and a vast stretch of wind-whipped water, over one of the broadest tidal reaches of the Thames.

There may be, among the bomb damage, some remains of Bricklayers' Arms Station (1840), long demoted, like Nine Elms, to a goods depot. Bricklayers' Arms was known as the "West End Terminus" of the South Eastern Railway and marks probably the first and last time the Old Kent Road has been described as the West End of London. It was a classic structure.

Somewhere, too, among arches, goods yards and stables down a side street off Shoreditch one may still be able to find remains of the old Terminus of the Eastern Union Railway (1839) which was designed by Sancton Wood. It was the precursor of Liverpool Street and its architect was a pupil of Sir Robert Smirke and like his master a bold classicist. He designed the palatial Roman terminus of Kingsbridge, Dublin (1845), with its twin cupolas, and Leinster Square, Paddington, and part of Hyde Park Gardens.

By the 'fifties, the old coaching view of railways was out of date.

They were establishing an architecture of their own and as keenly as Tractarians and Evangelicals they joined in the Battle of the Styles, Classic *v.* Gothic. On the whole the Classic style won. Euston, long a pioneer in railway architecture, set the tone with the Euston Great Hall which was completed in 1849. It was the joint design of old Philip Hardwick and his son Philip Charles Hardwick. Never had there been and never has there been since in England so magnificent a piece of railway architecture. This huge hall is now ruined with filthy little kiosks and enquiry bureaux built in a jazz-modern style by the L.M.S. But not even these destroy its proportions and it is still possible to note its double staircase, its rich ceiling, its figured consols supporting the ceiling and carved by John Thomas, who made the figures and bosses in the Houses of Parliament. At the top of the staircase, and not open to the public, is the room for the Shareholders' General Meetings, an untouched specimen of Roman Revival of the late 'forties. This sumptuous hall and offices set the fashion for railway architecture. Even the chairs of waiting rooms and desks in the offices had a Roman grandeur about them, executed in oak and mahogany, solid and heavy as a Christmas dinner. To compare with Euston, there is nothing. Other lines as they built their termini and chief suburban stations went in for classic, but the classic style preferred was that of the French Renaissance. It may be seen in those stations of the 'sixties, Charing Cross, Cannon Street, Broad Street, Farringdon Street, Aldersgate, Highbury, Bow, Camden Town, and it even survived into the next decade when Holborn Viaduct Station was built.

The architect of Charing Cross and Cannon Street was Edward Middleton Barry, a son of Sir Charles, the architect of the Houses of Parliament. Edward's masterpiece is undoubtedly the Charing Cross Hotel (1864). I know few pleasanter meeting places than the first floor of that building. A broad staircase leads to corridors done in the manner of Sir John Soane, unexpectedly Graeco-Roman when there is so much French Renaissance about the exterior. On this floor is the suite of rooms I call "the club." There is a smoking room with bar attached and billiard room adjoining and one can walk on to a balcony, drink in hand, to survey the crowds and trains of the station below. There are horse-hair seats in the smoking room, a bookshelf with a set of Shakespeare and a guide to the Southern Railway, and one has the place to oneself, while all around in stately dining rooms, private luncheons are being held by old-fashioned boards of directors, the Ouse Catchment Board, the Blackwall Tunnel Company, the Tower Hamlets Development Society, the United Kingdom Union of Persecuting Protestants. Much of this activity used to occur at the Cannon Street Hotel (1866) designed by the same architect. The station itself at Cannon Street is a far finer building than that at Charing Cross which has been deprived of its original semi-circular roof. Barry's towers and cupolas at the river opening of Cannon Street compare well with Wren's steeples and blend this great structure into the steepled outline of the City.

The only time the Great Western went in for Classic in a big way was when it employed Philip Charles Hardwick to design the Paddington Hotel in the 'sixties. The dining room here with its curving caryatids, probably by John Thomas, was almost up to the standard of Euston's Graeco-Roman office buildings. Just before the Hitler war this dining room, or "Coffee Room" as it was called, was ruined by being streamlined with plywood in a jazz-modern manner, so that it is now like any semi-smart new restaurant. The Great Western otherwise has been fairly loyal to Tudor, a style which it first adopted at Temple Meads, Bristol, and still employs there. The only nearly untouched examples of a Tudor station on the London to Bristol line which survive are Shrivenham and Box. There was an unfortunate period in the nineteen-thirties when the Great Western went "Modern" in the Great West Road sense of that word, with its new office buildings at Paddington. It adopted at this time too that hideous monogram on its engines. When Paddington Station was rebuilt the company employed Digby Wyatt on architectural effects.

The richest Gothic station is, of course, St. Pancras (1868). The enormous iron and glass roof with a clear span of 240 feet, 100 feet high and 700 feet long, makes the trains and platforms below it look like a model railway. It was designed by P. W. Barlow, the Civil Engineer. The tie beams that hold it are below the station and form a roof for the enormous vaults, which are under the whole area of the station. The hotel which is attached to the station, but not related to it, is by Sir Gilbert Scott. Ferguson much objected to it. "There is no proportion between the shed and its uses, and everything looks out of place, and most of all the Gothic mouldings and brick work, borrowed from the domestic architecture of the Middle Ages, which thrusts itself between the gigantic iron ribs of the roof."

Ferguson did not like the Gothic Revival, and even Sir Gilbert does not seem to have been wholly enthusiastic about St. Pancras Hotel. Never one to underestimate his own work, he says of it: "My own belief is that it is possibly *too good* for its purpose, but having been disappointed, through Lord Palmerston, of my ardent hope of carrying out my style in the Government offices, and the subject having been in the meanwhile taken out of my hands by other architects, I was glad to be able to erect one building in that style in London."

The hotel is now, alas, offices. But the splendid intertwining double staircase of ironwork survives (in the well of this there used to be a Turkish kiosk for coffee) and the huge Arthurian style wallpapers are to be found here and there. The refreshment rooms have all been jazzed and only the station booking hall remains as an untouched Scott interior. Alongside St. Pancras is the Midland goods station whose brickwork is undoubtedly the best in London. Sir Gilbert, like his grandson Sir Giles, was always interested in brick and stonework and for the goods station he had bricks specially made of varying sizes. You may see in the screen wall of the building (with its exquisite iron

82

grilles) that the bricks grow smaller as they go higher, giving an effect of solidity to the wall.

Of the exterior of the hotel I am myself enamoured. The clock tower has always seemed to be a highly picturesque outline and the rows of middle-pointed windows along the whole curving sweep achieve an effect of unity with diversity. As a practical plan for an hotel, the building is appalling. But as an exercise in scale and the skilful use of brick and stone it is unsurpassed in railway architecture. All other Midland stations in London are an anti-climax, as though the company had ruined itself on St. Pancras and had to be content with mere wooden sheds and brick booking halls for the rest of the system. Fenchurch Street, which it took over from the London, Tilbury and Southend Railway, is a humbler affair more in the manner of (and but a few years later than) the Great Northern Railway terminus of King's Cross.

This building, which Ferguson describes as the more successful and pleasing "plainer sister" of St. Pancras, is entirely the work of the engineer Joseph Cubitt. It was built in 1851 and the materials are white brick, glass and iron. The purpose at once is plain. One great semi-circular archway is for departure, the other beside it is for arrival. Between them on the main front is appropriately placed a clock tower. A colonnade of brick arches runs along the base of this front, between vast brick buttresses, and acts as a shelter for those awaiting their carriages. The booking office is on the departure side of the building and opposite this is a crescent-shaped hotel in a simple white-brick and stone, classic style. Office buildings balance this on the arrival side of the station. The coherence of the design is now much hampered by an underground station and by shops which hide its truthful simplicity from the Euston Road. Ruskin said in the *Seven Lamps of Architecture*, "Better bury gold in the embankments than put it in ornaments on the stations . . . Railroad architecture has, or would have, a dignity of its own, if it were only left to its work. You would not put rings on the fingers of a smith at his anvil." He must surely have approved King's Cross, though he makes no specific mention of it. It is certainly the only London station which is pure railway architecture. I have always thought the new Underground stations (except that at Hammersmith) self-consciously simple in comparison with King's Cross. They are so much aware that they are in the "modern style," so tastefully arranged with red brick on the street level, and so streamlined that they smack more of the advertising agency than the railway.

King's Cross started no new style, except at different stations on its own line beyond London. The nearest approach to it, other than Fenchurch Street, is Liverpool Street which was built in the 'seventies. It is civil engineer's Gothic, rather than architect's Gothic, and none the worse for that. The Gothic-style iron pillars support many-vistaed arcading, the flattened arch of the roof is crenelated on its own hanging edge and many mouldings and capitals in ironwork are to be found by the careful observer. Indeed, on a foggy evening, when those pear-shaped arc lamps used to hang down low from the roof, casting a purplish-white light, Liverpool Street had quite a resemblance to an ancient abbey.

The last large station to be built in London was Marylebone (1899) for the Great Central Railway. Its buildings are of hard pink midland bricks with yellow terra-cotta dressings and all in Flemish Renaissance style. They look like a public library from Nottingham which has unexpectedly found itself in London. A beautiful description of this station and of the Great Central Railway is to be found in Mr. Hamilton Ellis's *The Trains We Loved*. The weakness of the Great Central for gorgeous decorations in its carriages did not extend to stations; but its luxury is commemorated in Colonel Edis's gorgeous Great Central Hotel on the Marylebone Road. This entirely dwarfs the quiet terminus behind it.

There is no doubt that Marylebone set a new tone to London

Railway architecture. Henceforward something more tasteful than the flimsy wooden constructions was considered suitable for suburban stations. The L. & N.W.R. employed the noted domestic architect Gerald Horsley in 1901 to design stations at Harrow and Pinner in a style half-way between that of a bank and a medium-sized country house. Harrow, with its tower, was remarkably successful. Termini were thought to be ornate in the wrong sort of way, too like the Louvre and not enough like Michael Angelo. So there were the great rebuildings in an Edwardian monumental Renaissance manner starting with the L.B. & S.C. in 1908 at Victoria. The most ponderous effort of all was Waterloo with its twenty-three platforms and vast, useless entrance arch, approached by flights of steps unlike Euston, symbolical of nothing. Baker Street by Charles W. Clarke was a quieter rebuilding for the Metropolitan Railway in the neo-Georgian style (1914). Its refreshment rooms are still untouched. The most charming of all the Edwardian and neo-Georgian Renaissance stations is the entrance to Charing Cross Underground by H. W. Ford (1913). Marble columns in restaurants, stained glass, thick and crinkly, and adorned with wreaths, Turkey carpets, bronze or beaten copper electroliers, mahogany screens with panels of bevelled glass, plaster-work in the baroque manner, external sculpture in the manner of Sir Hamo Thorneycroft as at Waterloo—all these are characteristic of the last age of Railway Architecture. Redecorations in this manner went on in nearly every station. The hotel at Liverpool Street sustained such refittings and even at the St. Pancras Hotel a dining room was redecorated in a "Georgian" style.

Such is the stylistic development of the London railways until the dismal grouping and the even more dismal eclipse of all individuality which has now occurred. But just as in a church architecture is not so important as the worship which goes on there, so in railways the associations of a station and of a line are part of its beauty. The personality of most stations in London survives, even through British

Railways, and will continue to do so until everyone in England is exactly the same as everyone else.

Waterloo is the "services" and race-goers' station—for "Pompey," "Soton," Aldershot, Epsom, Ascot. It has a rather high-class suburban connection. Civil Servants who have reached C.M.G. and knighthood stage find it near Whitehall and convenient for Esher and in pine-clad Southern Electric suburbs their wives play cards with wives of rich city gentlemen. The humbler Civil Servant uses the Metropolitan and moves outwards beyond to Rickmansworth and Northwood as his salary increases. He probably knows he is not going to reach the heights of Esher Civil Servants and there is no point in establishing a railway carriage connection on the Southern Electric. The commercial people who use the Metropolitan are in their turn slightly less rich than the city gentlemen who use Waterloo.

The flashiest of all suburban travellers are those who travel daily from Victoria by first-class Pullman trains to Brighton. Indeed, Brighton so dominates Victoria Station that though continental trains depart from its South Eastern Section, though many of the inner London suburbs are served by puzzling loop lines which start here and end at London Bridge, Victoria is the station of what moneyed leisure is left in London. Though it is meant to be associated with the South Coast and summer holidays, the sea is not what one associates with those who use it regularly. They do not look as though they took a winter dip in the English Channel. Warm flats, television, cocktail cabinets and bridge seem to be more in their line.

What a contrast is Liverpool Street! Here those extraordinary, cramped and uncomfortable Great Eastern carriages are drawn out above the East End housetops to wide acres of Essex suburb, two-storey houses, flat recreation grounds, strange chapels of strange sects, the well-trodden commons on the fringes of Epping Forest. Here workmen's trains run early in the morning. Here the old London sulphur smell pervades and even red bricks receive a black coating.

Dense streets of Tottenham, Wanstead, Leytonstone, Barking, Edmonton, you are the real London and you form a barrier between the town and the unspoiled country of East Anglia! So many trains carry your patient passengers in and out of the black cathedral of Liverpool Street that expresses to Harwich, Yarmouth and Norwich seem slow at starting and ending for fear, no doubt, of knocking into one of these hundreds of suburban steam trains. Fenchurch Street has the same quality as Liverpool Street and so has London Bridge.

Charing Cross is the railway's concession to the Continent. Though it is possible to leave Charing Cross for Kent, the impression travellers like to give when they use Charing Cross is that they are going abroad. Little Bureaux de Change at the entrance encourage the impression and Edward Middleton Barry's elaborate Eleanor Cross, befouled by pigeons in the station yard, reminds us once more of one of Europe's shining gifts to England, Eleanor of Castile.

I do not know what to say of Cannon Street. Of all the stations of London it is my favourite, so echoing, so lofty and so sad. Whoever used it and who uses it now? Holborn Viaduct was the great station for hop-pickers on their journey to Kent. But Cannon Street is too stately for that sort of thing. It is much less important than London Bridge at which most of its trains stop. Perhaps the people of Bromley, that lonely high-class suburb in Kent, love Cannon Street as I do.

There is one station, however, which hardly anyone uses at all—Broad Street, which is given over to ghosts of frock-coated citizens who once crowded the old North London trains from the steam suburbs of Highbury, Canonbury and Camden Town. Often do those sumptuous L.M.S. electric trains swing across the North London suburbs on that smooth, useless, beautiful journey to Richmond. At no time of day have I known it impossible to find a seat in their spacious carriages. And the frock-coated ones are dead and gone like the rolling stock which carried them, their houses have been turned into flats, their gardens built over by factories. The North London was

87

the last line to use wooden-seated third-class carriages as it did on its Poplar branch (now closed), the last line in London to run no trains during church time on a Sunday morning, and within living memory the General Manager of the line refused to allow Smith's bookstall on Broad Street to sell any vulgar-looking papers. Still the trains run, through haunted gas-lit stations, on the most revealing railway journey London can provide.

The main line platforms of King's Cross are all expresses and Civil Servants bagging the first-class sleepers to Scotland, their fares paid for them out of our taxes. I do not like it, despite its noble architecture. It is a station, like Euston, that those few of us who are not Civil Servants will associate with injustice. But these dim suburban platforms at King's Cross to which trains come puffing up from the inner circle, are still Victorian London. Here runs much uncomfortable rolling stock to Barnet and Hatfield, climbing slowly to Finsbury Park. All the money is spent on streamlining those L.N.E.R. expresses in the main station.

St. Pancras is a station apart, a Royal Station. The old idea that the Midland was the most comfortable railway in the world still holds good despite the strenuous efforts of the L.M.S. to kill it. There is a suburban service, but it is of no importance. I have the impression that St. Pancras is still the aristocratic route to Scotland. Gun-cases and fishing-rods go north with tweed-clad lairds, salmon and game returning in the guard's van without them. I have little doubt that British Railways will do away with St. Pancras altogether. It is too beautiful and too romantic to survive. It is not of this age. Euston has stolen its trains but not its atmosphere. Except for that concealed platform where the Irish mail leaves of an evening, there is no personality left about the trains from Euston. To the Irish, Euston is the chief of English stations. Even lesser stations on the line are written on their minds for I know of an Irish Peer who woke up during a Wagner Opera at Covent Garden and exclaimed: "Just like Willesden Junction!"

Except for Broad Street, Marylebone is the quietest station. Only two expresses leave it in a day, the "South Yorkshireman" and the "Master Cutler." There is hardly room for more and the suburban service to Buckinghamshire seems like an after-thought. I have never met anyone who has used one of the Marylebone expresses, but lately I had the pleasure of coming into Marylebone on a semi-express which stopped at Brackley. We rushed through late Victorian cuttings and under bridges of glazed brick, nearly merging with the Metropolitan. When I reached London I found I was one of fifteen passengers.

Paddington has the strongest personality of all the larger London stations. Its passengers are nearly all country people. There is the one exception, a large contingent of South Welsh who seem always to be travelling in trains. There is a lessening section of old-fashioned people, too poor now to travel first, who come up on the cheap day fares from Wiltshire and Gloucestershire to visit the Army and Navy Stores. Relations from further west stay a night or two at the Paddington Hotel. There are some Oxford dons and at holiday times more schoolboys than on any other line. Add to them a final section of commuters who have transformed Newbury and Maidenhead, Reading and Henley into suburbs of London.

I am aware that this attempt at the atmosphere of London stations is sketchy. Sketchy and no doubt unfair, for there must be many to whom King's Cross and Euston are charming places and others who detest Cannon Street, St. Pancras and Liverpool Street as I do not. To them I apologise, but if I have caused them to think of these stations as places with the strong personalities that only those who use them can know, I will have achieved my object. To me they are people, and people have sides to their characters that they reveal to some and not to others.

10 NONCONFORMIST ARCHITECTURE

THE church of the medieval village or town was the centre of life. Houses were squalid and uncomfortable and it would have been as odd for a villager to say his daily prayers at home with all the family crawling about the single room, as it would be odd to find a villager saying his prayers on a week-day in the village church today. Church was where one went for everything. Schooling and business in the porch, festivals and plays in the church and churchyard, games in the churchyard (headstones in a graveyard were almost unknown until the seventeenth century and the poor were buried one on top of another in the graveyard, without a coffin, so that the quick danced upon the dead), and only the chancel and guild private chapels and priest's part were screened off from the noisy, much-used nave, the people's part of the church.

Nor were the guild chapels entirely apart from the people. The maltsters, let us say, of a district would erect an addition to their Church in honour of the patron saint of malting; they would subscribe for a window depicting the saint's life, less rich guilds would subscribe to keeping the candles burning, to a panel of stained glass, or a carved figure, or to part of the priest's stipend or the care or making of vestments. So it happened that the cottager of Catholic England looked on the church as his true home and took the same pride in his little bit of the church as he takes today in a new three-piece suite at home, or as his wife takes in the ornaments on her mantelpiece.

Churches really were the architecture of the people.

Since Elizabeth's day the church has become more and more remote, in architecture, from the people. The private chapel of the
squire's family became the squire's pew, and when the squire was sold
up in the last century it was cleared away by a "restorer" and became
an awkward corner of ill-placed seats filled only on harvest festival or
at the British Legion service. The rest of the church became the
province of the incumbent and many a country church today is little
more than an additional drawing-room for the rector's wife to which
the family at the manor has presented some new but ecclesiastical
ornaments.

Yet it is wrong to suppose that the Calvinism of Edward VI, the
Romanism of Mary, the compromise effected by Queen Elizabeth,
killed people's interest in God. The continual change in church
services, the destruction of many ornaments for which the people had
paid and which was part of their life, harmed the Catholic Church in
England, and Cromwell nearly killed it. But though they were no
longer full Catholics, people still talked a lot about God. In Cromwell's time they talked about Him in public-houses, at street corners, at
home, during business and everlastingly in Parliament. The translated Bible, full stops, commas, mistranslations and all, was open to
any who could read, and the pious English put their own interpretation
on various scriptural texts, counting one text as more important than
others. So arose Fifth Monarchy men, Muggletonians, Seventh Day
Baptists, Millenarians among the lesser Cromwellian sects, Independents [1] (now called Congregationalists), Presbyterians (now mostly
Unitarians in England), Baptists and Quakers among the greater.
A Catholic would say these sects arose because there was no Church
guidance in the interpretation of the scriptures. A Puritan would say
that now at last people could read the word of God.

It would be too sweeping to say that the early meeting houses
were that architecture of the people which had been driven out of

[1] The Independents started in England in the mid-sixteenth century.

the churches merely because the early Puritans were mostly intellectuals and their ministers clergy who had been ejected from their livings, displaced heads of colleges and scholars. The congregations, according to the Lambeth returns, consisted of a good sprinkling of landowners, schoolmasters and merchants. The earliest meeting places were cottages and larger private houses, for ministers and congregation expected to be replaced in the church at some change of government.

When the Restoration brought about a High Church reaction, and later when William III, the one and only Royal Calvinist, failed to insist that the Church of England was Presbyterian, Baptist or Independent, the dissenters started to move out from their cottage meetings and to build their own conventicles.

The earliest Nonconformist places of worship, built specifically for worship, are all later than 1650. They were designed as preaching houses.[1] Usually they are plain, often delicate, compositions with windows on three sides and the pulpit approached by steps against the fourth. Sometimes there is a clear space in the middle of the room, for a communion table. Galleries round three sides were often added.

In their simplest form, in the Quaker meeting houses where the doctrine of the Society demanded no worldly ostentation whatever, the buildings have the quality of a well-scoured farmhouse kitchen—a stone or tiled floor, scrubbed oak open seats, white walls and clear glass windows. Sometimes in the older meeting houses the walls were covered to the height of a man's shoulder with rush matting. One might say the Quakers were the Cistercians of Nonconformist builders. The Unitarians (then Presbyterians) were the Cluniacs. They did not despise decorative treatment, angels' heads as exterior keystones,

[1] It is interesting to notice Mr. F. Etchells' observation that Wren seems to have been aware of the double nature of the Church of England, its Laudian and Puritan sides, for while St. Paul's has space for a hundred altars and could be a Catholic place of worship, his City churches are often primarily preaching houses.

broken pediments, excellent brickwork. The Unitarian Year Book
gives the dates of the foundations of various churches, and where these
have not been rebuilt much excellent work is to be found.

Among the best Nonconformist churches of this first phase, what
we might call the theological style, are Friars' Street, Ipswich; Mary
Street, Taunton; Churchgate Street, Bury St. Edmunds; Underbank, Stannington; the Octagon, Norwich. All these have lavishly
furnished interiors, somewhat after the manner of a Wren church.

Of the buildings belonging to the Quakers, necessarily far simpler,
Jordans, near Beaconsfield, is probably the best example, though I
have attended numerous small country meetings where a scrubbed
and white-washed austerity still recalls the strictness of old Friends.

*Friars' Street, Ipswich. 1700. Plaster walls and white woodwork. This and the
following three chapels illustrated represent the theological style belonging to the convinced
phase of Nonconformity when it emerged from secret meetings and built its own
conventicles.*

The earliest Baptist churches, notably Cote, Oxon (1657), have the austerity of Friends' Meeting Houses.

The first Methodist preaching house was not built until 1739 in Bristol and it survives almost as it was, for Sir George Oately, the Bristol architect, has carried out a conservative and sensitive restoration of the old place. This building is the first of a larger series of chapels than that of the first group and I think we might name it the first building of the architecture of Enthusiasm.

Consider the difference between the motives for building Methodist

Underbank Stannington, nr. Sheffield.   1742.   Local grey stone.

chapels and those for building Unitarian, Independent, and even Bapist places of worship. The latter were built for congregations versed in theology, to hear the Word of God from Ministers who held similar views on the Word to those of the congregation.

When John Wesley died in 1791 there were 60,000 Methodists in Great Britain and 11,000 in Ireland; most of them were in the northern and western counties of England and in the north and east of Ireland. These people were mostly men who had not previously bothered about spiritual matters; they were workers from early and

Exterior and interior of Unitarian Chapel, Bury St. Edmunds. Early eighteenth-century. Dark red brick, white paint. Unitarians were intellectuals. They had no moral objections to decoration and built many lovely chapels with Wren-like exteriors and fine woodwork within. They were not allowed towers or spires.

Cote Baptist Chapel, nr. Bampton, Oxon. 1651. Grey limestone among the willows, elms and flat landscape of the upper Thames. Interior: high pews, white walls, gallery and clear glass. Neighbouring brooks and ponds suitable for baptism. The simplicity of these Puritan Chapels, built for people who believed and argued not for people who believed and sang or shouted praise, was deliberate.

dismal, industrial districts, half starved people who saw no hope of ease and happiness in this life and were attracted by the promises of indescribable ease and happiness in the next. Where Wesley or Whitfield lifted their voices, people fell down with groans and wrestled with the Evil One.

The first chapels to be built by the Methodists were meant to serve as overflow preaching houses when the Established church was either too far distant, too hostile, or too small in seating capacity for the numbers attracted by the new preaching. Like the buildings of the earlier group, they were designed to seat as many people as possible within a good view of the pulpit. Crosses, altars and decoration were regarded as unnecessary, for there were such things at the Parish

Lady Huntingdon Chapel, Worcester. An "enthusiastic" interior in a Chippendale Gothic style, with nineteenth-century liturgical movement additions. Clustered columns, cornices, gallery pews, buff, yellow and white paint, dark green walls, organ with stencilled pipes, stained glass and pulpit rails are Victorian. Entrance screens (not shown) have good early nineteenth-century coloured glass. This chapel belongs to the second phase of Nonconformity (Wesley and Whitfield) when the buildings often conform to classic rules of proportion and are indistinguishable externally from contemporary buildings of the Establishment.

church. They followed, in plan, the "theological" preaching houses, but they were larger, flimsier buildings, and did not scorn a bit of carpenter's or plasterer's moulding here and there by way of internal embellishment. They were erected mostly by pious merchants or landowners whose enthusiasm extended to their pockets. They were hardly any of them erected from the subscriptions of the people. Indeed enthusiasm in the late eighteenth century was as rife as

Louth, Lincs. Methodist, 1835. Small town Enthusiasm: not architect designed but by a builder with a Georgian tradition and some Adam-style casts. Windows not spoiled by cathedral glass of liturgical movement, two rows allow for gallery between first and second floors. Later it became customary to bring the galleries across the single long windows on entrance front to give a non-domestic appearance to the façade. This and the following five illustrations show the development of a native English style.

Blockley, Gloucestershire. 1835. The façade, except for the large windows and wide door, is in the Bath tradition which often survived as late and as far east as this.

Swaffham, Norfolk. Methodist c. 1870. Fanciful; a certain debt to Soane and Wightwick. White brick, frosted glass and bright coloured borders.

Market Harborough, Leicestershire, c. 1850.   White brick and pale yellow stucco.

Tractarianism was seventy years later and touched similar classes at the top, though it had a greater hold than Tractarianism over the people at the bottom of the social scale.

When great cities prospered after the depression following the Napoleonic wars, and Methodist merchants grew richer, stately chapels were built in the chastest Greek or Commissioner's Perpendicular. Liverpool, Manchester, London and Bristol still contain a number. But they were built at a time when education in architectural matters was confined to those classes which were rich enough to

Oundle. 1863. Grey limestone. It has the enormous pediment that became almost a hall mark of the mid-nineteenth-century chapel.

have an extensive education or to recognize established taste when they saw it. There was little to choose between an early nineteenth-century Methodist, New Jerusalem, Roman, Independent or Unitarian chapel in a large town (where most Nonconformist building at this time took place) and a Proprietary chapel or new chapel of ease erected for the Established Church. They did not have bells or towers, but their internal arrangements were similar. Enthusiasm was strong in parts of the Established Church. The pulpit dominated the altar. Several octagonal, circular, and hexagonal churches were built for the Establishment (the Octagon Chapel, Bath; the Octagon Chapel, Wisbech; St. Andrew's Church, Dublin—circular—and a dozen or more) while those which retained the rectangular plan, also favoured by Nonconformists, had exceedingly shallow chancels and the pulpit was more than often in front of the Table. On the Nonconformist side, there was an 'Established' look at, for example, the Wesleyan Chapel, Stanhope Street, Liverpool (c. 1820), where a contemporary account says "A powerful, fine wind organ, by Bewsher and Fleetwood, gives solemnity to the services; and the 'semireligious light' falling through an oval window of stained glass, executed by Messrs. Lyon & Son, imparts a sacred shade to the communion table."

The architecture of enthusiasm reflected the cultivated taste of a class which had not yet lost its authority. The difference from the Establishment was one of plan, and often that difference was slight.

Where, in the country and in small towns, there was less wealthy patronage for the enthusiastic chapels, the buildings were unpretentious and what the *Little Guides* would call "barn-like" structures, an epithet which those guides apply to many a not dissimilar late eighteenth-century church. By "barn-like" I mean serviceable structures obeying the traditional rules of proportion and solid craftsmanship to be found in all Builders' Assistants from *The Builder's Jewel*, to Nicholson. The interiors were often wholly delightful: pale pink walls, Chippendale Gothic ceilings, high grained-oak pews, white gallery fronts and double rows of clear glass sash-windows round three sides of the building, and against the blank fourth wall a fine mahogany pulpit, sometimes inlaid and moulded. The town of Bridport, Dorset, has two little-spoiled chapels of the enthusiastic period comprising several of the features.

At last we come to the most interesting phase of Nonconformist architecture, that which shows more surely than any Victorian

Donhead, Wilts. Methodist c. 1860. Chilmark stone with paler dressings, Soane-ish door and Gothic glazing bars.

Established church, whether high, low, broad, Gothic, Romanesque or Classic, what was the true architecture of the people. Not since medieval days had the people clubbed together to adorn a place of worship and this time it was not a shrine but a preaching house. In mining districts and lonely villages of Wales, among the gleaming granite and slate of Cornwall, down the brick-red streets of Leeds,

Belfast, Liverpool and Manchester, in almost every city and corrugated suburb of Great Britain and the Six Counties Area, wedged in on the common land beside country houses and red and blue among the thatched roofs of southern villages or the stone roofs of northern ones, stand the chapels of the mid-nineteenth century. Despised by architects, ignored by guide books, too briefly mentioned by directories, these variagated conventicles are witnesses of the taste of industrial Britain. They try to ape nothing. They were anxious not to look like the church, which held them in contempt; nor like a house, for they were places of worship; nor like a theatre, for they were sacred piles. They succeeded in looking like what they are—chapels, so that the most unobservant traveller can tell a chapel from any other building in the street.[1]

The nineteenth century was a period of great religious revivals and this is not the place to examine their causes. The chapels were built as the result of those revivals and they represent pennies saved which might otherwise have been spent on drink, or profits from tiny shops and lean farms and gardens where farm workers had toiled until sundown. They contain, more often than not, a social hall and schoolroom for the the many P.S.A. meetings, groups, Fellowships, prayers and study meetings which occur on every weekday in a thriving Nonconformist community. They are the public equivalent of the parlour mantelpiece. All sorts of people connected with the chapel contributed their bit; the local builder supplied the labour and the plan; the ironmonger the cast iron railings and the lamps; the timber merchant the wood; a builders' merchant gave of his best in ridge tiles, stonecaps and dressings; another builder undertook to look out coloured glass and window frames; carpenters in the congregation fixed the pews; painters did the graining and the stencilling; the linen draper looked to the cushions and coverings; and when it was all

[1] I only know of one exception—the Circus Church, Portsmouth (if it still stands), which looks Nonconformist but is very low Church of England.

Blaenconin, on the Cardigan=Narberth Road. c. 1830. This and the following illustra-tions belong to the Celtic tradition. There are far more chapels in Wales and Cornwall than in the rest of Britain. They are national emblems. The chief characteristics of Welsh chapels are a disregard of the established rules of proportion, very varied proportion for each building, though not much structural originality, and strong colour schemes.

finished the stationer at his own steam press produced the illustrated
account of the opening ceremony. Those who had no trade or craft
directly connected with the chapel subscribed all they could. Pitch
pine pews, green walls, brass, Lombardic and handsomely-painted
pulpit, lamp brackets, carpeted alleys, stencilled texts and homeliness—
it was better than the best house in the circuit. And yet it was built
more on the lines of a pre-Reformation Catholic church than the
correctest Pugin or boldest Butterfield. These were indeed the
thresholds of a better world than this, the brick and stone expression
of individual conversion and acceptance, not the stilted copying of a

*Belgelley, Pembrokeshire. 1866. Blue-grey walls with paler granite dressings; purple
brown door; slate roof.*

Between Cardigan and Aberayron.   Unusual composition for district.   A reckless and effective use of simple shades.   Pock-marked grey walls, mid-purple brown paint.

Kilgelley, Pembrokeshire. 1869.

religion based on Prayer Books and Missals and idol worship. This was the Liberal vote.

It would be a pleasure to try to trace some individuality of style belonging to each of the denominations of Nonconformity. But this is

Near Cardigan.   Classical arrangement with duplicated door.

possible only in the most general way. In England the five chief divisions are Methodist, Congregational, Baptist, Brethren and other denominations. Wales is a separate study and Scotland does not come within the scope of this article.

The Methodist church today is a Union of various Methodist Societies which sprang up so soon as Wesley's followers started to ordain their own ministers without the medium of a Bishop of the Church of England. The oldest were the Wesleyan Methodists and on the whole they were the richest. Their buildings, when they are not of the chaste, enthusiastic period, were rebuilt quite late in the nineteenth century and in a solid style generally faintly echoing the ancient Gothic style of the Established Church, externally at any rate.

The Primitive Methodists broke from the Wesleyans in 1810. They were humbler and more wildly enthusiastic people than the Wesleyans. They favoured camp meetings, female preachers, and the uttering of loud ejaculations during inspired prayers. By 1851 they had 3,000 chapels. Their architecture is very rarely Gothic; they are often tiny structures on waste spaces by the roadside in the country or high flimsy-looking Italianate barns in the towns. They employed architects more rarely than any other denomination.

The United Methodists arose in 1850 and were an amalgamation of various offshoots from the original society. Their buildings were humbler than those of the Wesleyans and abound in Cornwall and Durham.

Humbler too, but unclassifiable, are the buildings of the various other branches of Methodism, now united, except for Calvinistic, in the Methodist Church.

Congregational churches are definitely more easily identified than others. These churches have each their own government but belong to a central Union whose headquarters are the freestone Memorial Hall in Farringdon Street (1874). They are a survival of the original Independent churches of the seventeenth century and have preserved a certain traditionalism in their architecture, even in their later nineteenth-century buildings. Congregational churches are more sedate and less home-made looking than those of any other denomination. Often an architect was employed. The earliest ones of the seventeenth and eighteenth centuries in Somerset are imposing classic

Mawgan-in-Meneage, Cornwall. Methodist, c. 1830. Yellow-washed preaching house, pointed window and dark-grained oak door alone suggest a place of worship.

Mawgan-in-Meneage, Cornwall. Interior: Luxurious Lombardic Italianate woodwork. Table below the pulpit. Flowers are a twentieth-century innovation, herald of liturgical movement in much recent Nonconformity.

buildings. That at Frome is famous. Until about 1860 most Congregational churches were built in a classic style, a public-worship variation of the middle class villa of the date, running through from Greek to Roman and Italianate. Possibly because there was something traditional and respectable about Gothic towards the latter half of the last century, later Congregational churches are Gothic, and Basil Champneys' Mansfield College, Oxford (1889-90) is one of the best bits of Perpendicular Revival in that city.

The Baptists roused themselves in the late eighteenth century when they started their great missionary effort. The General Baptists (not to be confused with the Strict and Particular Baptists, who are small and Calvinistic) are the largest body of Nonconformists in the world and their largest following is in America. In England the Baptists made their greatest progress in the 1860's, when Spurgeon was one of the most famous men in England. They increased threefold. Their new churches had some of the traditionalism of the Congregationals. They usually built large classic conventicles of which that at Newington Butts was, as it were, the cathedral. Their architecture has never been sufficiently studied and it would be a good thing if the Baptist Historical Society were to produce a record of their chapels as thorough as that produced by the Unitarians.

Plymouth Brethren are one of the few Nonconformist bodies still increasing. They are divided among themselves, but their meeting places can be distinguished from others by the board which generally says

THE LORD'S DAY.

Breaking of Bread, 11 *a.m.*

The Gospel will be preached here (God Willing) 6.30 *p.m.*

The sect is of nineteenth-century origin and its buildings are a cross between the Quaker meeting house and the Primitive Methodist chapel.

Tisbury, Wiltshire. Methodist. A Nonconformist's answer to the Establishment's Gothic revival. A mixture of all Gothic styles in Chilmark stone, battleship grey. The Georgian traditions survive in the two-storey window arrangement for galleries and in the Church of Ireland pinnacles.

Louth, Lincolnshire. Congregational, c. 1885. Flamboyant solution of the gable problem, neither Gothic nor Italianate, but English. Red brick with stone dressings.

Other denominations in England, except the Quakers whose meeting houses remain resolutely unostentatious, are unclassifiable.[1]

In Wales the chapel architecture of the nineteenth century is not denominational but racial. It is hardly ever architect-designed, but the product of a local contractor who has made the fullest use of an illustrated catalogue. The congregations are often, to this day, in debt to the contractor for his work. The buildings are essentially local and vary with the districts. They have the quality of good sign-writing and a vigorous style of their own. In one the designer will

---

[1] I am not including the splendid buildings of the Catholic Apostolic Church under the heading of Nonconformist architecture.

Legbourne, Lincs.   Pale yellow brick with purple-brown railings.

*Broad Town, Wilts.   It looks as though it has been under water.   Grey-green plaster,
frosted glass with star-patterned borders and faded yellow plaster in the pediment of the
porch, railings red-lead colour.*

have concentrated on emphasising the windows, in another on bringing
out the texture of the stone, in another on arranging ingeniously the
doors and windows of the west front, in another on colouring the
outside plaster.   These buildings have beauty which is apart from
date and akin to the naïveté of the Douanier Rousseau.

Great Yarmouth. Methodist. Grandest native Baroque mixed-style unified by central arch which also modifies an otherwise top-heavy pediment.

Since about 1910 there has been a liturgical movement in many Nonconformist churches and this has affected new building. Unitarian churches now have chancels; Holy Tables have bunches of flowers on them and the pulpit is losing its old position of predominance. Even Methodist churches have a sober look and may be mistaken, externally, for a mission church of the Church of England. The two

118

styles usually adopted are either Perpendicular with a touch of *art-nouveau* and terra-cotta about it, or Christian Science Romanesque. Indeed the new buildings of Nonconformity lack the individuality and strong character of those scrubbed conventicles of the seventeenth and eighteenth centuries or the gigantic preaching houses of the Victorian age.

11 1837–1937

The Drift Towards Ugliness

THE history of the last hundred years of taste in England is profoundly influenced by three things : increase in population, mass production, absence of any uniting faith. The development of Boggleton, a small English town which I have traced at set periods in the next pages, is symptomatic of all England. We can learn the character of the country from the scars and wrinkles on its face. Probably no other place in Europe was so beautiful as England in 1820, few are uglier than it is round its larger towns today. In 1820 there were high standards of craftsmanship and certain canons of taste. Today craftsmanship has gone, or is revived, without any appreciable influence, by escapists. Canons of taste are as uncertain as they are various.

The history of Boggleton may help to show how this has come about and for those who prefer their art history in terms of generalisations, I have summarised each section with some general remarks.

1837

It is interesting to analyse, as one enters an English provincial town today, the statement that no error of taste was committed before 1840 and to consider how far it is true.

A provincial town presents a complete history of nineteenth-century taste which is still traceable underneath the hoardings, neon signs and wires with which progress has strung every feature of urban and even rural landscape. And there is no doubt that architecture is the outward and visible form of inward and spiritual grace or disgrace. So it is with architecture. I propose to start this account.

The topographical dictionary (1837) describes Boggleton as a neat market-town standing in an elevated position on the slopes of the Bogdown hills. The subsoil is limestone. The population is 3,000. The chief industries are flint knapping, for flint-lock muskets, and agriculture. There is a decent town hall recently erected (1825); an ancient Parish Church situated not far from the centre of the town, an Independent Chapel and a Meeting House for the Society of Friends in Bowling Green Alley. Magnificent views are obtainable from the Common, a considerable expanse to the south to which freeholders have had the right of free pasturage since the time of King John.

And what the topographical dictionary omits, the eye of the traveller will discern as he bowls through the main street in his coach and four, putting up at *The Dolphin* where there is adequate stabling for his horses.

The main street of Boggleton is of even appearance. It is wide and well-proportioned and the Doric columns of the new Town Hall make a fine termination to the vista which the traveller sees as he approaches from London.

On either side of the Town Hall are the more considerable shops, each with square-paned windows and a uniform style of lettering above them in gold. Plain Georgian houses rise above the shop fronts, the windows on the first floor being larger than those on the second and those on the second being larger than those on the top. The roofs are hidden by a low parapet. The material of the houses is mostly limestone, but the Town Hall and *The Dolphin* which are larger than any other buildings in the street, are of white brick from the recently opened brick-fields outside the town. They are plain but imposing edifices whose beauty depends on that subtlety of proportion which all architects of the late Georgian era had learned from the close study of

Greek art and its adaptation to modern buildings, as expressed in the lectures of Sir John Soane. Breaking the uniform grey of these substantial buildings in limestone and plaster or white brick is a large, mellow red-brick mansion, the thick white glazing bars of whose windows, the subtle classical stone-carving of whose keystones, cornices and dressings, the heavy solidity of whose panelled front door, coupled with the absence of any sign of commerce in the way of shop front or sign, betrays the presence of some wealthy person of private means. This is Adamsbec House, the town residence of the Adamsbecs, whose large country estate and house is some distance away. The family rarely comes to it now since the improved method of highway travel has brought the Metropolis within nearer reach.

Except for this cluster of buildings round the centre of the town, Boggleton will not present much of architectural interest to the traveller of 1837.

The rest of the High Street diminishes London-wards into what are little more than stone cottages, some of them bulging with bow-windowed shop fronts or standing apart to admit a glimpse of the meadows to the south and the elm-clad hills to the north of the town. Down one of these alleys is the Quaker Meeting House, a simple affair in limestone with scrubbed benches and white walls within and nicely graded tiled roof distinguishing its plain exterior. The Independent Chapel is also a plain building (1794) resembling, with its two storeys of round-headed windows, a thin private house. It is a little more obtrusive than the Quaker Meeting House, since it was put up after the persecution of Nonconformists and dares to show itself in the High Street.

The ancient Parish Church will attract the traveller's antiquarian but not his æsthetic attention. It is an irregular building in the late-pointed style. It stands a little distance behind the Town Hall and is surrounded by alleys between cottages, some of which are built of clunch and clearly very ancient, though scarcely genteel. The church, indeed, stands in the old centre of the town and the cottages round it are a survival, built in the haphazard medieval way of growing, of the village which Boggleton was before it became an agricultural centre, for Boggleton was never a planned medieval city within walls. The citizens objected to their Common being used for sales, so a site north of the church was used for bargaining, where the road entered the village. This was built round and gradually became the market place and new centre of Boggleton life.[1]

The interior of the Parish Church presents a venerable appearance. An elaborately carved wooden screen runs across the chancel and north chapel. The walls are whitewashed and form a handsome gallery of hatchments and mural monuments. Some of the latter were done by a talented stonemason in the town from a book of engravings for mural monuments published by I. Taylor in 1787. The pews are of good deal and comfortable, being of excellent joinery with well-fitting doors. The cushions in them are of watered silk and one pew at least has a stove in it which warms Mr. Awdon and his family, merchant and Mayor of the town. There is a west gallery for the choir whose instruments are kept there out of the way of the ringers below. The three-decker pulpit is used by the now ageing incumbent who cele-brates quarterly Communion.

Having inspected the church and refreshed himself, the coachman and horses, the traveller, will pass on towards Adamsbecton, the large country house of the Adamsbec family. About a mile out of the town, the ruins of Godley Abbey, rise up among the willows and elms of the valley. The pile is a monument to superstition but, at the same time, it has much of the sublime, seeming to draw towards it the surrounding hills.

A row of genteel houses looks on the abbey from the further side of the road. These are airy and cheerful, having been built in 1820.

[1] This is by no means the only reason for the market place being here. Mystery plays, and later fairs, were held near this space.

They are in a variety of styles. One in Grecian with a wide verandah commanding the prospect, the other is something like it but plainer and of three storeys with a balcony of elegant ironwork on the first floor. The third is called the Oratory and is in the Gothic taste with pointed windows and an octagonal parlour, a veritable monkish cell. This is nearer the abbey than the other two houses, and is calculated to blend in with that structure. The houses are inhabited by a retired merchant, a retired naval captain, the younger son of a family whose fortunes have declined and two maiden ladies, daughters of a former rector of Boggleton.

Our traveller will now have little to attract him after this glimpse of the picturesque until he comes to Adamsbecton. There he will be permitted to see the gallery which contains a Salvator Rosa, a Lawrence, a Reynolds, three Lelys, a Murillo, a Canaletto and a Guido Reni, as well as several paintings of the Dutch school and even more of the Italian schools.

The people of Boggleton take their town for granted, just as our traveller takes the hospitality of Adamsbecton for granted. Carpenters, masons and builders are good craftsmen and an architect building in the district can rely on them to do their work well and supply the appropriate mouldings in the specified places. Merchants are unhampered by undue rivalry and the farmers are prosperous. The gentry are, many of them, liberal. Only some, the meaner sort of persons, have cause for complaint.

The Last Days of Tradition

The most significant thing about the arts of this time was not the usual clash between classic and romantic, but the tradition of craftsmanship which pervaded everything from the mouldings round the lintel of a door to the title page of a book.

The machine was getting into its stride, but the British tradition of thoroughness had not yet died out. The knowledge of detail inherited from a system of apprenticeship appears in the exquisite bindings of books, the high standard of engraving, the chaste layout of the typographer. No work was skimped. Even the speculative builder had a civic conscience and laid out several stuccoed estates round our larger towns which for spaciousness of planning and æsthetic beauty have yet to be improved upon in our own era of town-planning.

The classic and romantic clash must certainly be considered. The classic comes first and there is no doubt that its greatest exponent was Sir John Soane, who invented a severe style of architecture which is the envy of every European country except its own. Artists of all sorts still went on the Grand Tour and those who could not afford it made careful drawings of classical sculpture, notably the Elgin marbles. There were certain dogmatic rules laid down for art. Traditional forms and compositions pervaded everything. Art criticism was, mercifully, in its infancy and had not yet reduced many a talented craftsman to a state of gittering self-consciousness.

Literature was almost entirely in the hands of the Romantic school. Coleridge, Southey and Wordsworth were established poets. Byron was a hero. Sentimental *Keepsake* annuals flooded the bookshops. Thomas Moore and Alaric A. Watts were drawing-room idols. Sir Walter Scott gave an impetus to reviving Gothic architecture which was far greater than that given by the whimsicalities of Walpole and Beckford. The popular style for the newest fashionable architecture was Perpendicular. In painting, this taste is expressed in the works of Cattermole and Joseph Nash and Prout. Scholars were taking to British antiquarianism.

1867

Just when it looked as though Boggleton was going to become one of those decayed market towns which would have been no credit to an age of progress and prosperity like the mid-nineteenth century, fortune saved it from oblivion. The Great Junction Railway decided that a site near Boggleton was a suitable place for its works. So in 1850 a town was built called New Boggleton. This consisted at first of several rows of workmen's dwellings with a central green space, a church, an institute and some shops.

Enterprising Boggletonians from the old town erected an arcade of shops at the edge of the new town. A farmer sold off his land to a speculator who proceeded to erect as many houses on it as he could fit in. Then there were no town-planning laws to stop him. New Boggleton spread until it met Old Boggleton and the small houses at the London end of the High Street came down under the onward rush of the new town.

The new works were a magnificent sight : a glimpse into the engine rooms showed vista upon vista of machines with men toiling happily at them. The G.J.R. built a huge viaduct across the valley outside the town. The old naval captain in one of the genteel houses by the Abbey—he was the last survivor of the original inhabitants of the group—thought that the viaduct was magnificent, comparable to the Abbey itself, symbolising the strength and beauty of engineering in cast iron and brick against the architecture of the Middle Ages. But he was a sensible man always in touch with the times.

The new rector (High Church: instituted a weekly Communion instead of the old quarterly administration of the Sacrament) was deeply opposed to the building of the viaduct. He tried to agitate with the Mayor and Corporation. But they were all for humouring the railway since big profits were to be made out of it. Only a few landowners sympathised with the rector and agreed that the viaduct ruined the venerable and picturesque appearance of the Abbey. So the rector had to content himself with medievalising his Parish Church. The old box pews were taken down and nice sticky pitch-pine ones of a Christian shape substituted. The windows were filled with coloured glass from Hardman's works. The screen across the chancel and north chapel was removed because it blocked the view of the new _chancel. The high pulpit was destroyed and a new one made out of the remains of the screen. The hatchments were removed and the plaster stripped from the walls.

The Nonconformists were no less active. But since the Established Church liked Gothic, they preferred the Italian style. The new Independent Chapel, now called Congregational, was of white brick with red brick dressings and in an ornate but inexpensive Romanesque manner.

The Adamsbec family had long ago sold Boggleton House to a prosperous shop-owner who gutted the interior and built warehouses in the garden. Plate glass took the place of the old square-paned windows and only a few of the more old-fashioned tradesmen who were unable to keep up with the new influx and increased competition regretted the passing of old Boggleton.

The railway brought with it newer manufactories, and more chapels and churches sprung up. On the hills outside the town a smartish suburb was built for the foremen and higher clerical people connected with the factories. The richest people of all built themselves huge country houses near the town: houses in the Jacobean style and the Italian style with high walls and iron gates with lamp-posts on either side of the drive and a crest on the top of each. One of the most prosperous of these rich men founded the Boggleton Art Gallery, which has some of the largest pictures in England on its walls depicting Crimean scenes, Highland cattle, historical occasions and various other subjects calculated to turn the minds of Boggleton mechanics from the contemplation of the machinery and urban scenery by which they were surrounded.

Old Boggleton and New Boggleton became a large town of 100,000 inhabitants and the only remains of Old Boggleton were the Town Hall and the Quaker Meeting House, while some cottages near the church still survived in a derelict condition as a memorial to the oldest Boggleton of all.

The Machine Gets into its Stride

The tradition of craftsmanship was supplanted by the machine. The Great Exhibition of 1851 had shown that many objects could be made by machine at a quarter the cost and just as well as those made by hand. The set rules of colour and design pervading in 1836 had not been forgotten and the exhibits of 1851 in the late-lamented Crystal Palace were still worthy of the study of the fastidious. It is fashionable now to laugh at the Great Exhibition. It is a pity that this humour does not extend to the exhibits displayed today in the windows of the multiple stores.

While the machine was still a symbol of progress (whatever progress might be) to the majority, it was terrifying to many intellectuals. The Oxford Movement in the Church had given Gothic architecture official approval. Gothic was medieval. The Middle Ages were the days of craftsmen and Christianity. Therefore the machine was un-Christian. Classical architecture was pagan. Individuality was sacred. Pugin and, later, Ruskin supported this reaction from the machine. The pre-Raphælites, now established, were the men of the moment. Art had caught up with literature. Even railway stations were built in the medieval style. The Grand Tour was supplanted by a visit to Belgium and the Gothic cathedrals of France. Venetian Gothic was imitated even in the main streets of London.

1907

About this time the Radicals in the town decided to improve the lot of the workers in the packed streets down by the railway works and other factories. An Evening Institute was founded, built in the New Art Style of Gothic (by the architect of the new Wesleyan Church). Lectures were given on the ruined Abbey (which was carefully patched up and the grass round it mowed and planted with beds of geraniums, a small admission fee being charged), on Italian painting, socialism, eugenics, eurythmics, hygiene, economics and other important subjects. The old cottages near the church were rebuilt in an even more ancient style than they had been in before.

The Conservatives decided to improve the civic dignity of Boggleton. The plain town hall was pulled down and a handsome edifice in Portland stone and in the Viennese Baroque manner arose in its place, surmounted by a tower with illuminated clock faces.

Ivy was planted along the buttresses of the railway viaduct to make it harmonise with the Abbey. The false stucco villas by the Abbey were at last taken down : a terrace of houses was put up by a speculator on a site nearer the Abbey itself, so that they would have commanded no view, anyway. The tram service was extended to the Abbey gates.

The rector's wife was an artistic woman and taught blob work (water-colours) in the Institute and sent her daughters to Bedales. The Municipal Art Gallery made her and her daughters laugh.

Boggleton had changed the colour of its buildings, just as it had changed the colour of its politics, to pink. Only the Quaker Meeting House remained the same.

The Morris Movement

The Classical tradition never died. Greek in 1837, Italianate in 1867, "Queen Anne" (Norman Shaw) in 1897, neo-Renaissance (Blomfield, Sir Ernest George, Belcher, Alfred Drury and various other sculptors of public monuments) in 1907.

The Gothic revival transmogrified itself. There could be too much medievalism. William Morris realised that the movement needed a political as well as a religious background. Guild socialism was the result. But Morris's insistence on hand processes, though often admirable for those rich enough to afford the price, led to various repulsive imitations. Sham beams, sham lanterns, sham Morris wallpapers spread rapidly. The productions of the Kelmscott Press, never legible, did little good to the few lingering traditions of English printing and typography. To counterbalance these bad effects, the Morris movement really did stimulate reaction to and criticism of many machine-made products, particularly furniture. The movement simplified designs and insisted on the simple life. From it sprang the Garden Cities, the C. F. A. Voysey, early Lutyens and Baillie Scott small houses, and later the Art Nouveau Movement. Daring radicalism, fresh air, the works of H. G. Wells, unstained oak, white nurseries, child welfare work. There was no hint of the Oxford Movement about the new Gothic revival. Much more a hint of free thought.

The *art nouveau* people are responsible for contemporary architecture at its best. George Walton and C. R. Mackintosh, who came from the famous Glasgow School, built in a style which was soon taken up in Germany. Only in its decorative features, such as ironwork and stencilling, did their architecture seem any different from the truly modern architecture of today.[1] It is ironic that the simplicity of the Crystal Palace should have been reached out of a movement indirectly inspired by that Gothic revival which was, in its inception, inimical to the machine age which the Palace glorified.

1937

Boggleton's period of prosperity was nearly over when orders for armaments brought temporary relief to some of the factories. The Adamsbecs have sold their country house as a building estate : their pictures fetched very little. The trams have been replaced by buses. Two of the Nonconformist Chapels have been sold to chain stores. The Bedalian daughters of the late rector have opened an "olde" tea place in one of the cottages near the church. The big merchants' houses outside the town have become a lunatic asylum, a hospital and municipal offices. Their grounds have been turned into a public park.

The population is being moved out of the crowded streets near the

[1] I now see that this is not true. *L'art nouveau* was a romantic escape into simplicity. Mackintosh's beautifully drawn houses are Beardsley-esque Scottish Baronial (*see* p. 176).

station.   Some are being moved into council houses put up on a nice but rather waterlogged site near the Abbey.   Others who can afford it are going into some of the lovely new villas which are being erected all round the town.   Each one is different, the beams being very cleverly arranged.   Stained-glass windows may be found in all of them, parlour or non-parlour type.   True the walls are thin, the wood of the doors is unseasoned, the foundations are bad, the chimneys smoke, there is not enough accommodation, but, on the other hand, every garden has a low wall and crazy paving, and the interior fittings are in an up-to-date jazz modern style.

There are hardly any prosperous local tradesmen as the big shops are all run by London combines.   Motors have brought prosperity to the Georgian *Dolphin Hotel*, which has rebuilt itself in the Tudor style in order to keep up with the times.

The Institute is not doing so well now that culture comes via the wireless and cinema.

I am afraid we have not much time for art in Boggleton, though art criticism is quite popular with some of us.   A Frank Brangwyn of a steel works was bought out of trust money by the Committee of the Municipal Art Gallery, but it was thought a little old-fashioned. Several young artists have been painting the viaduct for their Commercial Art course.   The Boggleton Surrealist has found the large canvases in the Art Gallery interesting.   Art, like the rest of the town, is controlled from London; there is no distinctive native talent, just as there is now no native craftsmanship.

Boggleton itself takes up much more room than it should do.   In 1837 you could see the meadows and elms between the houses in the High Street, now you will have to go at least a mile in any direction to see a tree at all—and even then the fields will have a municipal appearance and the burnt grass will be bright with pieces of paper.

12 VICTORIAN ARCHITECTURE

VICTORIAN BUILDINGS will never become as smart as Georgian ones are today. Georgian architecture is the last product of a settled agricultural civilisation when craftsmanship was understood and enjoyed, and rules of proportion were widely known among builders. The jerry-building of Georgian industrialism has hardly survived, and where it does exist, as at Coalbrookdale and here and there in the older industrial towns of the North and in the Stroud valley in Gloucestershire, people who look at it do not think of it as "Georgian" but as simple and dateless. Most of what is Georgian that survives is well-made and easy to look at. Our minds carry in them a coloured aquatint, be it landscape or street, to form a suitable background to a Georgian building. Then Georgian is nicely and cheaply faked. Blocks of flats, all London over, have Regency beds and Brighton-Pavilion curtains, out of scale with the cupboard-like rooms in which they are placed, no doubt, but unmistakably Georgian. Even an estate agent knows what Georgian means, and I have seen the word used in terms of praise of a house in a serial in *The Symbol*, the paper that is bound up with our parish magazine.

But Victorian can never be smart. It will even defy the analysis of the "doctors" busy classifying everything around us. You have to use your eyes when looking at it.

Much Victorian architecture is really bad and shoddy. That famous drawing of Doré's is a true condemnation of much Victorian industrial building. A modern Doré, I should add, could equally condemn our own jerry-building in the period between the wars and in the present glorious age of prefabs.

I think the chief objections to Victorian architecture are being overcome by time. No one likes the architecture of his immediate predecessors, and most of the writers of architectural books are the children of Victorian parents. Indeed, most widely-read writers from H. G. Wells and John Galsworthy to Berta Ruck and Denise Robins, are writers of the age of reaction from Victorianism. They like few ornaments, plain walls, pastel shades, open windows and as little decoration as possible, or, if there *is* any, a sort of diluted Swedish such as may be bought at Heal's. Again, twenty years ago, young men prided themselves on having social consciences rather than æsthetic perception. Victorian building was utterly condemned and stood in their minds for back-to-back houses in Leeds and those soulless stacks of Dwellings for Artisans which were built with the idea of class distinction. And oh! how horrible class distinction seemed to be in those class-conscious days twenty years ago.

The Victorians very much enjoyed decoration, and decoration in the 'thirties was considered immoral. The Tower Bridge was the symbol of all that was sentimental and therefore wicked.

Finally, Victorians were condemned for not planning. But this last condemnation is based on ignorance. There are throughout England industrial estates very carefully planned, as well as middle-class and upper-class neighbourhoods which now may well have become slums owing to the poverty of our people, but which in those days were not so drab as modern town planners' brochures like to make them appear.

On the credit side, the Victorians were allowed to have produced some good buildings provided no architect had been near them. Civil engineers were, we were told, the great Victorian architects. The Crystal Palace was the first prefab, and this is quite true. Engineering triumphs by Brunel, Stevenson and Barlow were photographed and admired. Cubitt's King's Cross Station, London (1851), was preferred in all its stark simplicity to the romantic outlines of Gilbert Scott's St. Pancras Hotel. And here we may say that the functionalists were echoing opinions expressed seventy years before by Ruskin.

But can it really be that the Victorian age in England which produced such great poets and artists produced no architects? Of course it is not true. And the way to look at Victorian architecture is to look at it in terms of architects. In former days, even in Georgian times, there were regional styles, and the style predominated over the man who wielded it. The builder was capable of being an architect and had more say in building and finishing an architect's design than he had in the nineteenth century, when architecture became a conscious profession. Builders thereafter did their best to imitate architects, but they rarely produced anything remarkable as a work of art except here and there in the building of mills and factories.

So in this most exciting of all architectural adventures—the hunt for what is good in Victorian brick and stone and iron—we move from the world of the dilettante and his craftsmen to the drawing rooms, clubs and studios of professional gentlemen. Talk is of the Battle of the Styles and of this man's new church and that man's town hall. So-and-So's son and So-and-So's pupil are watched with interest. The centre of architectural activity is now London, and London men go by train all over England at the behest of rich Liberal merchants and Tractarian landowners. Sir Gilbert Scott finds himself away in the Midlands and telegraphs to his office "Why am I here?" It was no unusual thing in those days for one London architect to be doing thirty large buildings at once. They had their equivalents, these great London men, in certain of the bigger provincial cities: the Worthingtons in Manchester, Pilkington, a Gothic Revival architect of real merit, in Edinburgh, Fulford in Exeter, Ordish in Leicester, and so on. But primarily it is London that is the centre, and I will now flick over with you an album of some of the drawings of these great men and talk a little as we watch the Battle of the Styles.

First there was the Classic Survival, a fine Graeco-Roman style suitable for London Clubs, Town Halls and the Head Offices of Banks. The noblest Classic Survival buildings are, I think, Goldsmith's Hall, London (P. Hardwick, 1829–35); St. George's Hall, Liverpool (H. L. Elmes, 1841); Euston Great Hall (P. Hardwick, 1840–7), and the work from the 'sixties until the 'eighties by J. Gibson for the National Provincial Bank. There are also the scholarly works of C. R. Cockerell for the Bank of England, and there is his Ashmolean and Taylorian building at Oxford. We might tack on to the Classic Survival the Byzantine Revival which may be seen in Christ Church, Streatham Hill, by Wild (1841), and that strange church by Sir William Tite at Gerrard's Cross (1859), and Pollen's University Church in Dublin (1858).

The Classic Survival is like a grand after-dinner speech, full of wisdom and elegant oratory. It goes with the port and brandy and the leather arm-chairs and the great velvet curtains of the London and provincial clubs and the station hotel. But the young men are not listening. They have turned from Greece and Rome to their own island, to chancel, screen and organ loft, to reredos and stoup. Some are led by the romance of medievalism to the Church of Rome; some continue to follow Pusey. The Gothic Revival of Queen Victoria's reign is all mixed up with social morality and religion which were deep concerns of educated people in those days.

Perhaps the most disastrous influence on the Gothic Revival was that of Pugin, because he it was, and not Ruskin, who said that no building was Christian unless it had a pointed arch. He was a lonely genius, a craftsman interested in detail and with an eye for colour and material and decoration. One feels that he was more interested in detail than structure. The plan and the grouping of the towers of the Houses of Parliament are Sir Charles Barry's, though the delicate decoration is Pugin's. I do not think it fair that Pugin should be given all the credit, as he now is, for Barry's building. Pugin could produce lovely buildings such as his Roman Catholic Cathedral at Birmingham, where he had not too much money. But his followers brought discredit on the Gothic Revival.

Sir Gilbert Scott, for instance, is a Pugin architect, and he it was who carried out Pugin's ideas to extreme lengths, insisting on Gothic for all occasions except on that great day when Palmerston finally thwarted his attempts to gothicise Whitehall. Pugin's books of Gothic detail and the many books that followed, giving mouldings and bosses and ball flowers and sedilia and even windows and doors suitable for domestic Gothic—these were a gift to the industrious copyist. Why England is filled with dull churches imitating medieval churches in Northamptonshire, Rutland and Oxon, may be put down to Pugin and later to Parker's *Glossary of Gothic Architecture* and those books of examples which I have mentioned. So long as a building was exactly like some medieval one in style, it was all right. And that chief Gothic stylist, Sir Gilbert Scott, was a man who, for all the 700 and more buildings that he designed, produced comparatively few which were original. Masonry and sound roofs and correct mouldings, he and his often more talented assistants employed. But Gothic to them was a style, not a way of building.

There were, it is true, one or two medievalists who produced enormous imitations of old styles which had a dignity, spaciousness and grandeur equal to, even if slightly and unaccountably different from, their precedents. The Catholic Apostolic Church in Gordon Square, London, by the brothers Brandon (1855), and Lancing College chapel by Carpenter (1854), are the best examples of the pure medievalist architecture in the Pugin tradition that I know. The work of Pugin's sons and successors has, I think, always been a little over-elaborate and lacking in proportion.

But the Gothic Revival architects of the 'fifties and 'sixties who should be taken most seriously are those whom Professor Lethaby used to describe as "hards," saying that their work was founded on building, on materials and ways of workmanship and proceeded by experiment. "One group I would call the 'softs,' the other the 'hards'; the former were primarily sketchers of 'designs,' the others thinkers and constructors."

The "hard" architects are few and great, and the three most remarkable pioneers who thought and constructed in Gothic rather than imitated, were William Butterfield (1814–1900), George Edmund Street (1824–81) and J. L. Pearson (1817–98). They were men of convinced Tractarian opinions. Their religion pervaded their work. They were more interested, certainly at the beginning of their careers, in constructing and "thinking in Gothic," as George Truefitt described it, than in style.

Butterfield in 1849 produced a church made out of bricks (All Saints, Margaret Street, London), and realising that bricks could not be carved like stone, he decorated his blank surfaces with coloured bricks, using little decoration at the base of his brick buildings and more towards the top. All his buildings are thoughtful, many of them inspired; none of them is like any medieval building anyone has ever seen. Butterfield worked on the principle that, since he was building in an age when workmen knew how to use brick and cast iron, he would build in brick and cast iron where those materials were most easily come by. In those parts of the West Country where stone was easily available, he used stone.

George Edmund Street was primarily a country architect, and his simple village schools and chapels-of-ease and convents in the Oxford Diocese are examples of Gothic continuing rather than Gothic revived. He followed the principles of construction which he found in old barns and farm buildings and applied them to the simple new churches he built in local materials.

Pearson was primarily interested in vaulting and thrust and

counter thrust.   He was almost entirely a church architect and his tall, narrow, stone and brick vaulted interiors are seen at their best at St. Augustine's, Kilburn (1871), St. Stephen's, Bournemouth, the Catholic Apostolic Church, Paddington, and Truro Cathedral.   These architects built for the glory of God.   Street alone of them seems, towards the end of his life, to have been slightly affected by the world and to have produced less interesting works, though his later work, the Law Courts, will impress everyone for its many-vista-ed thoughtfulness.

Other " hards " whose work will be admired by anyone who bothers to look at them are James Brooks—St. Columba's, Haggerston; St. Chad's, Haggerston; St. John's, Holland Road, Kensington: William Burges—St. Finbar's Cathedral, Cork; a house in Melbury Road, Kensington; the Speech Hall, Harrow School: E. G. Paley, a North of England architect: J. P. Seddon—University of Wales, Aberystwyth: S. S. Teulon—St. Stephen's, Haverstock Hill, London: William White —All Saints', Notting Hill; St. Saviour's, Highbury, London: Henry Woodyer—St. Michael's, Tenbury; St. Paul's, Wokingham; New Schools, Eton.

Hard or soft, these Victorian architects were often an inspiration to their pupils.   Mr. Street's office seems to have been a very gay place. When William Morris, Edmund Sedding, who was known as " Jaggy Baggy," Norman Shaw, known as Corporal Bullfoot, and J. D. Sedding were in the office in Oxford, there was one pupil there named Hayward who stuttered.   He sang better than he spoke, so it became the custom to chant to him in Gregorian plainsong through rolled-up foolscap.   On Ascension Day Mr. Street gave them the day off, provided they went to church, remarking, " Some of you, I know, have voices."   Life in Scott's office was equally gay, for the Master was away getting jobs much of the time and he talked very good sense to his pupils.   Butterfield's office, however, cannot have been a very enjoyable place.   He never entered his drawing office himself, the late Harry Redfern who was articled to him tells us, and referred to his draughtsmen as clerks. Butterfield himself, looking rather like Glad-stone, sat silent in an adjoining room and his clerks would bring their drawings in to him, which he corrected in ink much to their annoyance. No holidays were allowed except church holidays, no smoking of course and only when he had left his Adelphi office for the Athenæum did his clerks dare to go out for lunch. The extreme churchiness of these great Tractarian architects produced reactions in their pupils and children. George Gilbert Scott junior, the eldest son of old Sir Gilbert and father of Sir Giles, became a Roman Catholic soon after his father's death. Possibly, as a kind of revenge on the usual copying of his father, he became one of the most original of the later architects of the Victorian age. In 1877 he designed St. Agnes, Kennington (now bombed), in a brick perpendicular style unheard of at that time and imitated everywhere for the next sixty years. Unlike his father, George Gilbert Scott junior defended the Classic style and was instru-mental in saving the decent brick classic parish church of Hampstead. He added an east end to Sir Christopher Wren's chapel at Pembroke College, Cambridge, which I think enhances the look of the chapel and is in exact keeping with Wren's style.

George Gilbert Scott's friend G. F. Bodley, another pupil from Scott's office, designed some churches in the manner of St. Agnes, Kennington, of which I particularly remember Hoar Cross, Stafford-shire; Holy Trinity, Kensington Gore; the Cowley Fathers' church, Oxford, and St. German's, Roath, Cardiff. A pupil of young Scott's was Temple Moore, who produced a beautiful, long, limpid perpen-dicular style partly his own and partly, it seems, Bodley's and the younger Scott's. The best examples of his work I know are St. Wilfrid's, Harrogate; All Saints', Basingstoke; All Saints', Tooting, and Pusey House, Oxford.

From Street's office emerged the most influential and attractive of all Victorian architects—Richard Norman Shaw (1831–1912). He was not a church architect. "I am a house man," he used to say to

Sedding, "and soil pipes are my speciality." The church which he designed at Bedford Park (1876–7), that early attempt at a garden city which owes its inspiration to Shaw, lacks mystery, but his secular buildings are unexampled. He started as a designer of Tudor-style houses such as "Leys Wood," Sussex (1868), and "Wispers," Midhurst (1875), making full use of tall external chimneys, half-timber gables and irregular sites. And then in 1873 he electrified the Metropolis by building the New Zealand Chambers in Leadenhall Street, City, in what was for some weird reason called "the Queen Anne style" but was in reality a form of Dutch Renaissance. He invented a façade for narrow city streets, which let in plenty of light and yet was neighbourly as street architecture. Thereafter he built much in a style more nearly approaching Queen Anne, and a foretaste of Lutyens, both small houses and large. Perhaps the best is 170 Queen's Gate, just near Colcutt's beautiful Imperial Institute. Other good works of his are Swan House, Chelsea (1876); Greenham Lodge, Newbury (1879), and New Scotland Yard (1887). Shaw was primarily interested in the purpose of a building and in the materials and methods of construction. Style was almost an afterthought. It was through thinking like this that he designed New Zealand Chambers and the town houses and offices for which his name will always be remembered. Shaw, more than anyone, was the originator of the small, simple, suburban house which first flourished in garden cities and has now reached local councils and official architects. Men who admired Shaw were first J. J. Stevenson and E. R. Robson, who designed the London council schools, and later Voysey, Baillie Scott, Leonard Stokes, Ernest George, Edwin Lutyens, Edgar Wood and the Tugwells, who built modest villas harmonising with the countryside, and individual in style. Shaw, indeed, was the founder of modern English architecture as we know it at its domestic best. Towards the end of his life he said that, if he were still in practice as an architect, he would be using concrete. And, indeed, he did use concrete construction of a most daring kind never seen in England before, when he built the convent for our Church of England Sisters of Bethany at Bournemouth in 1874.

One of Shaw's closest friends was J. D. Sedding, a church architect whose work still seems modern whether it is Classic or Gothic. He designed Holy Redeemer, Clerkenwell (1888), and Holy Trinity, Sloane Street, London (1890). Shaw, Stevenson, Godwin, Sedding, George Gilbert Scott junior, Bodley and their followers represent the traditional English styles coming through Gothic Revival and out again into the open. They are the product of the arts and crafts movement and they are not escapists. They were interested in plan and material, both of the house itself and of every detail in the house, and from that some of them moved on into the planning of towns as a whole, but such men were rarely successful as domestic architects.

There were one or two freaks at the end of the last century whose work is fascinating, but outside the main stream. W. H. Crossland, for instance, in 1887, having been sent round to the châteaux of France by Joseph Holloway (the maker of Holloway's Female Pills), came back and designed that outsize château in red brick and Portland stone called Holloway College on the fir-clad heights above Egham. Beresford Pite, a sound architect and beautiful artist, won the Soane Medallion in 1880 for a design for a West-End club house in a Wagnerian Gothic style that exceeded the wildest fancies of the earlier Gothic Revivalists. Some architects, such as Henry T. Hare and T. G. Jackson (Anglo Jackson), went in for the early Renaissance manner, others went in for a sort of Beardsley-esque baronial. The chief protagonists of this style were two great architects, C. R. Mackintosh and George Walton. They are wrongly, I think, heralded as pioneers of modern architecture. They now seem to me to belong to the *art nouveau* of the 1890's and I associate them with the early work of Charles Holden. Their ecclesiastical expression is to be found in Caröe's strange *art nouveau* church of St. David at Exeter.

It has been hard trying to survey the juxtaposition of personalities and styles of Victorian architecture in one article. The subject is so much a matter of individuals. Trends and tastes are but surface ripples and end in journalistic generalisations, of which there is already far too much in what I have written. I would advise anyone who is interested in architecture, be it Victorian or Georgian, to look at some of the works of the great men I have mentioned here. There are bound to be examples within twenty or thirty miles of every reader, in England at any rate, and very often the work of these men extended abroad.

Look at the buildings first; remembering if you are struck with horror and amazement that the Victorians had all the courage of their convictions and, more often than not, a disregard for texture and dislike of what they thought "late" or "debased," that is to say the perpendicular Gothic and, later in the century, the Greek Revival classic style. Having looked, tried to sympathise, sifted good from pretentious, then is the time to read the stimulating works of those pioneers in the appreciation of Victorian building, Mr. Goodhart-Rendel, Sir Kenneth Clark and Mr. John Summerson.

ILLUSTRATED NOTES TO VICTORIAN ARCHITECTURE

1 *South London, 1872*

BUILDING NOT ARCHITECTURE. This view of crowded houses [1] between viaducts of South London is by Gustave Doré from his *London* (1872). It is no
more Victorian architecture than Metroland is modern architecture. It is
merely building, and it gives the Victorians a bad name. It is hurried development of houses for artisans built as near their work as possible. Today prefabs
are built further from work, because today the motor car, not the railway,
determines the siting of buildings. But are prefabs better? Victorians were
a class-conscious people and artisans' dwellings, middle-class dwellings and
gentlemen's residences were accepted standards of housing. One climbed
or sank according to capabilities from one class to another.

2   *King's Cross Station, 1851, by Lewis Cubitt*

3   *York Central Station, c. 1890*

ENGINEERING. Victorian railway engineers with their viaducts, tunnel entrances and stations produced many fine additions to the landscape. Steam added dignity where the internal combustion engine has only brought squalor. King's Cross Station [2], built in 1851 from designs of a civil engineer, Lewis Cubitt, is a simple building in London brick scarcely visible today because of a conglomeration of trivial building in front of it. It expresses its purpose clearly enough: one arch is the departure side and the other is the arrival side. A colonnade serves to protect people alighting from or entering carriages.

This view of York Central Station [3] is a late Victorian photograph. The ironwork is by Butler & Sons of Leeds. It is of four spans of 55 feet and is 795 feet long. The cathedral-like beauty is fortuitous, except that Gothic is often engineering in stone and this is engineering in iron. It is, however, a mistake to confuse æsthetics with morality, to say that because a thing expresses its purpose it is *ipso facto* beautiful. Much depends on the purpose. Cathedrals were built to the glory of God when men believed in Him. Stations like York were built for railways when railways were admired and Britain was still proud of her craftsmanship and confident in material progress. Much modern public building is the product of unconfident committees of taste, such as the Royal Fine Arts Commission.

4   *St. George's Hall, Liverpool, 1841, by H. L. Elmes*

145

THE CLASSIC SURVIVAL went on right through the Victorian age. It is a scholarly elaboration of the Greek Revival into Græco-Roman and Roman and even Baroque. For the most part it is the Conservative style and goes with big clubs, velvet curtains, municipal dinners, vintage port and good manners. One of its finest expositions is St. George's Hall, Liverpool [4], designed by H. L. Elmes in 1841, who died before it was finished.

THE CLASSIC SURVIVAL was maintained by many architects, such as C. R. Cockerell, Tite, Brodrick of Leeds, Pennethorne and "Greek" Thomson. John Gibson, Sir Charles Barry's pupil, built most of the National Provincial Banks in Great Britain and this example at Sunderland [5], 1878 is one of his last. It is full-blown Italianate adapted to commercial purposes.

5   *National Provincial Bank, Sunderland, 1878, by John Gibson*

THE GOTHIC REVIVAL.   Victorian architects did not consider themselves as either gentlemen amateurs like Wren or as builders, as they did a century or more earlier. They had become "professional" and not trades-people, just as doctors had ceased to be "apothecaries" and lawyers mere "attorneys." The Royal Institute of British Architects was founded in 1837.   Henceforth the interest in architecture shifts from regional styles and builders to individuals.

6 *Catholic Apostolic Church, Gordon Square, London, 1855, by Raphael Brandon*

7 *Lancing Chapel, Sussex, 1854–1870, by R. C. and R. H. Carpenter and W. Slater*

Who was in who's office mattered and whether he was a Classic or a Gothic man.   London men received many provincial jobs.   Local styles disappeared in favour of individual styles by the big men.   Without a doubt the more vigorous men were in favour of Gothic.   There were the pure medievalists who believed Pugin's false and then attractive dictum that the only Christian styles were the ones with a pointed arch.   The Gothicists sunk themselves into the medieval dream of that eccentric and persuasive genius, whose accomplishment is usually less impressive than that of his followers.   Raphael Brandon, who designed the superb Catholic Apostolic Church [6], Gordon Square, London, in 1855, was a medievalist.   He and his brother produced standard works on roofs and Gothic ornament drawn and measured from English examples.   They piled the fruit of their learning one on top of another so that Salisbury, Lichfield, Lincoln and Carlisle Cathedrals contribute details which support a hammerbeam roof of East Anglian type.   The whole is welded together by an exquisite sense of proportion not so apparent in their other works.   But this noble Gordon Square church for a beautiful liturgy is copying Gothic rather than thinking in it.

THE MEDIEVALISTS, looking back to Pugin's dream of the past, usually met with the approval of the Camden Society in the Church.   They favoured Middle Pointed or Decorated, considered the most "perfect," as opposed to Early Pointed or Early English, considered the most "pure."   Perpendicular or late pointed was called "debased."   Generally Camdenians copied, but they sometimes produced buildings as fine as any medieval one and except for texture hardly distinguishable from the medieval.   R. C. Carpenter, his son R. H. Carpenter and their partner W. Slater built Lancing Chapel [7], Sussex, 1854–70, which is one of the best medievalist buildings.

THE SUCCESSFUL COPYIST was Sir Gilbert Scott, who had the biggest practice any one architect has ever enjoyed in Britain.   He had a large office and talented staff and could himself design some severely handsome buildings, as in his additions to Bradfield Church, Berks, and his new church of St. Anne, Alderney, and he could be bold, as in the Albert Memorial, and use picturesque outline, as in his St. Pancras Hotel, London.   But he thought of Gothic as a "style" and his staff turned out impressive designs to please committees.   At the end of his life he designed the Rathaus at Hamburg [8], in the once popular Middle-Pointed style.   But lest he should not win the competition for which his drawing was entered, he produced another elevation in Flemish Renaissance [9].   A true Gothic building could not so easily change its face.   Scott often stands for "façadism."

J. L. Pearson was a medievalist, who in the middle of his long life (1817–97) turned to French Gothic and produced an Early English of his own

8   *The Rathaus, Hamburg, 1878, by Sir Gilbert Scott*

9   *Alternative design for the Rathaus, Hamburg, by Sir Gilbert Scott*

with brick-vaulting and stone ribs, which is ingenious and learned, producing many vistas of aisles tunnelled through external buttresses. The best example, St. John's, Red Lion Square, London [10], was destroyed by the Nazis. But St. Augustine's, Kilburn, the Catholic Apostolic Church, Maida Vale, London,

10   *St. John the Evangelist, Red Lion Square, London, 1874–1878, by J. L. Pearson*

and the stone built Truro Cathedral and St. Stephen's, Bournemouth, survive. So does his beautiful early church of St. Peter's, Vauxhall, London. He was primarily a church architect and a devout Tractarian, as were the majority of the best Gothic men—Street, Butterfield, Bodley, Brooks and Micklethwaite.

RUSKINIAN GOTHIC was a way of "thinking in Gothic." Ruskin, though not interested for long in the English Gothic Revival and then chiefly in Street, was instrumental in securing Benjamin Woodward to design the University Museum, Oxford [11] in 1852–55. It is the Oxford plan of a quadrangle

11   *University Museum, Oxford, 1852–1855, by Benjamin Woodward*

with a deep plinth and a fine gate tower. The Glastonbury-kitchen style appendage was for lecture halls and laboratories. The workmen themselves decorated the buildings with carving. By comparison Meadow Buildings, Christ Church, by Woodward's partner, Deane, is a wretched affair with its showy jumble of picturesque and unrelated features.

"THE HARDS." Of Mid-Victorian architects W. R. Lethaby writes, "One group turns to imitation, style 'effects,' paper designs and exhibition; the other founds on building, on materials and ways of workmanship and proceeds by experiment. One group I would call the Softs, the other the Hards; the former were primarily sketchers and exhibitors of 'designs,' the others thinkers and constructors." William Burges was an early and eccentric "Hard" who built a medieval world round him of jokes and pet animals and gorgeous colours. But he was also a sound constructor. He drew in bistre on vellum, as in these drawings for Cardiff Castle [12]. The house he built for himself in Melbury Road, Kensington (1870–81), survives with much of its original decoration [13]. It is a vision of reds and golds and coloured marbles, a Soane Museum interpreted in terms of Burges's own square Gothic. He also

12 *Drawings for Cardiff Castle, 1865, by William Burges*

13 *William Burges's house, Melbury Road, Kensington, 1870–1881*

14 *All Saints', Margaret Street, London, 1849–1850, by William Butterfield*

designed Harrow School Speech Room, St. Finbar's Cathedral, Cork, Brisbane
Cathedral and the east end of Waltham Abbey.

WILLIAM BUTTERFIELD (1814–1900) was an austere Tractarian and the
most original architect of his time. He looked like Gladstone. He built All
Saints', Margaret Street, London, 1849–50 [14], in brick. That was because
he believed that in a brick age you should use the material the workmen were
then wont to use. He had his own brick Gothic style, not a copy of medieval
but a development from it. His chief surviving buildings, besides this one, are
St. Augustine's College, Canterbury, Perth Cathedral and Rugby Chapel. A
severe small country church of his which is the essence of Butterfield is that at
Milton, near Banbury. He was, unlike most Victorian architects, a sensitive
restorer of old churches, cf. Ottery St. Mary, Shottesbrooke, and Tottenham.
Butterfield never produced drawings to attract clients. They took him or left
him. His "clerks," as he called his pupils, drew for him in pencil. He corrected the drawings in ink and they had to start afresh. Scaffolding was
dusted before he arrived on the site. These drawings sent to his builders,

Drawing for Keble College Chapel, Oxford, 1876, by William Butterfield

16 *St. Columba's, Haggerston, London, 1867–1869, by James Brooks*

Purnells of Rugby, for Keble College Chapel, 1876, are for brick, since Keble is in the brick suburb of North Oxford with which it harmonises. The drawing [15] shows the principles of his use of coloured brick. A general Victorian principle was that Gothic is more elaborate the nearer it reaches Heaven. This Butterfield followed. But he also emphasised construction. Where there is a heavy downward pressure at the base the lines are few and horizontal and strongly marked. When the wall is a screen wall only, as above the East window, he uses chequer pattern. Roof thrusts are indicated by criss-cross pattern.

A follower of Butterfield was James Brooks, who built what Lethaby called "big-boned churches" for London in stock bricks. St. Columba's, Haggerston, London, 1867–69, is a good example [16]. A rich chancel, whose height is emphasised by low nave arcades and whose beauty is enhanced by brick vaulting, leads the eye to the centre of Tractarian worship, the altar. Tractarians did not hold with more than one altar in a church and that visible from all parts of it. Light was to come from a large west window to fall on books, since this was a literate generation which used books and needed to see them.

The most genial and active and influential of the "hard" architects was George Edmund Street (1824–81), who was in Scott's office and then set up as a church architect first in Cornwall and next in the Diocese of Oxford at Wantage. He was a great craftsman and loved ironwork, masonry, needlework and joinery. All his churches are carefully detailed and he saw to all this himself. William Morris, Philip Webb, Norman Shaw and J. D. Sedding were all in his office and caught his enthusiasm. He was an uncompromising Gothicist and his domestic work was always in local material and handled with great sense of massing, as at Cuddesdon Theological College, Oxford [17].

17   *Cuddesdon Theological College, Oxford, 1853–1854, by G. E. Street*

Street believed in sketching all the time and was a rapid draughtsman himself, as in this sketch of his of the ambulatory at St. Julien at Brioude, France [18]. His books on Spanish and North Italian Gothic are still standard works.

18   *Sketch by G. E. Street of St. Julien, Brioude, France*

Street died comparatively young while still at work on the Law Courts, London. His small simple buildings such as his village schools in Berkshire and his chapels of ease as that at Westcott, Bucks, had a perfection of proportion and good use of local stone which was never so well caught by any other architect then or since.   His restorations were heavy-handed, but a fine large work of his was the Nave at Bristol Cathedral [19], where he continued the ingenious medieval scheme of the choir, putting tall windows in the aisle and lighting the nave from them.

Another "hard," almost too hard to be enjoyable, was Alfred Waterhouse,

19   *Bristol Cathedral, restoration by G. E. Street 1868–1888*

whose best works are undoubtedly Manchester Town Hall, 1877 [20] and Assize Courts, 1859. He was a clever planner and had little respect for local material or styles or textures. The ugly part of Caius College, Cambridge, on Kings Parade, is his and so are Balliol College, Oxford, and the Prudential Insurance Building, Holborn, and the Gower Street Hospital, London. But like the other "hards," he thought in Gothic and did not copy.

20 *Manchester Town Hall, 1877, by Alfred Waterhouse*

THE YOUNG MEN FROM MR. STREET'S OFFICE founded good modern housing. The greatest of them was Norman Shaw (1831-1912), who is described by Sir Edwin Lutyens as the greatest architect since Wren. "I'm a house man," he used to say, "not a church man, and soil pipes are my speciality." The comfortable modern house of the day is largely due to Norman Shaw, so are many modern methods of construction with reinforced concrete, which he used before anyone else. Shaw electrified the metropolis by building an office block, New Zealand Chambers [21], in 1872 in the City of London. He hit on a method of admitting as much daylight as possible into an office in a narrow

21   *New Zealand Chambers, London, 1872, by Norman Shaw*

street. This building was destroyed by the Nazis. The style was called "Queen Anne," and Shaw built houses in the style in Fitzjohn's Avenue, Hampstead, and for merchant princes all over England. He varied it with

22   *Design for Devonshire Street, E.C.2, 1877, by W. West Neve*

Tudor. His "Queen Anne" style was usually a neighbourly decoration for well-lit and practical commercial or domestic buildings. New Zealand Chambers reduced to its bare essentials, as in the design of 1877 by West Neve in Devonshire Street, E.C.2 [22], is a foretaste of the modern simpler style of today.

It is as well to see how domestic architecture seems of a different world compared with that of less than a century before. Here is a late eighteenth-century residence in Dublin, Charlemont House [23], designed by Lord Charlemont and Sir William Chambers. It exemplifies all the eighteenth-century characteristics: the rusticated ground floor, the large rooms on the

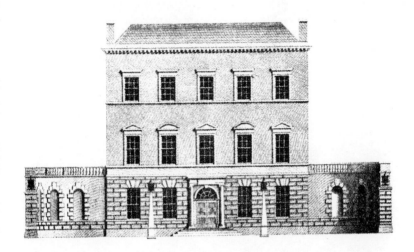

23   *Charlemont House, Dublin, c. 1773, by Lord Charlemont and Sir William Chambers*

first floor, a decent space before the smaller windows of the bedroom **storey**, the glazing bars of the windows related to the proportions of the windows, the windows related to the wall, a parapet concealing the attics. All is symmetrical even to the chimneys, which stand rather awkwardly at the sides like a pair of ears. Such a design, simpler or more elaborate, and varying a little according to local materials and methods of masonry and glazing, would look elegant anywhere and Georgian always. Now compare Norman Shaw's "Wispers," Midhurst, Sussex [24], 1875. This is no Gothic façade to a classic building nor stucco-Tudor of the late Georgian or early Victorian St. John's Wood or Leamington variety. It is not even a classic structure with superb late Gothic adornment, like the Houses of Parliament. It is related to its uneven site, it is conceived in masses, the chimneys are made into features instead of appendages, it is built in a traditional domestic style, both modern and Tudor. It may be the great-aunt of much fake olde-worlde, but it is not built as a fake. The arrangement of chimneys and roofs Shaw learned from Street.

24 *"Wispers", Midhurst, Sussex, 1875, by Norman Shaw*

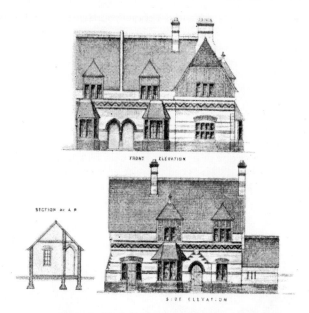

FRONT ELEVATION

SECTION at A B

SIDE ELEVATION

25   *House in North Oxford, 1870, by Clapton C. Rolfe*

Even greater was Shaw's influence on the small house. Here is a pleasant enough artisan dwelling [25] by Clapton C. Rolfe in North Oxford, 1870. It is in the polychrome style of Butterfield. Compare it with Norman Shaw's Hostelry [26] for that first garden suburb he laid out at Bedford Park, London

"The STORES"   Private House   Jᴱ Hostelry

26   *Hostelry, Bedford Park, London, 1878, by Norman Shaw*

(1878), and we are out of the Victorian era into a manner of building we have seen in our own lifetime.

Norman Shaw's influence on domestic architecture was enormous. He and Morris might equally be described as founders of the Arts and Crafts movement. Shaw's houses had Morris papers. Shaw believed in using local styles and local builders and whenever he found old craftsmen he employed them. His followers, such as C. F. A. Voysey, M. H. Baillie Scott and Edgar Wood, built houses of a strongly individual but yet hand-wrought and local-looking style. They tried to make cottages for the middle classes in the old cottage style and designed their own fabrics and furniture. Indeed Voysey continued his architecture down to the very toast racks and spoons, as Burges had done before him. Edgar Wood's cottage at Rochdale [27] is a Yorkshire example. It may be arty-crafty, but it is serviceable and does no violence to the landscape. H. L. North of Bangor was a Welsh Edgar Wood.

27   *Cottage at Rochdale, 1895, by Edgar Wood*

What Shaw was to small houses, George Gilbert Scott, Junior, Sir Gilbert Scott's eldest son and the father of Sir Giles Gilbert Scott, was to new churches. In 1877 he built St. Agnes, Kennington [28]. It caused great controversy as it was built of brick in the Perpendicular style then thought "debased." The nave arcades had no capitals to their columns, there was a screen across the chancel arch and provision was made for side chapels. The glass was by Kempe. St. Agnes was destroyed by the Nazis, as was Scott's All Hallows, Southwark. But St. Mark's Milverton, Leamington, and St. Augustine's,

28 *St. Agnes, Kennington, 1877, by George Gilbert Scott, junior*

Hull, survive as work of this great architect's Neo-Perpendicular manner. He was as much at home with the Renaissance style.

Two years earlier F. C. Deshon had designed this Mission Church [29] in a style that was then thought "debased" because it had no pointed arches and was unashamedly structural.

Within the image: *Design for a Missionary Chapel.*

29   *Mission Church, 1875, by F. C. Deshon*

30   *Church of the Holy Angels, Hoar Cross, 1877, by G. F. Bodley*

G. F. Bodley, a pupil of the older Scott and a close friend of the younger Scott, designed Holy Angels Church, Hoar Cross, in 1877 [30]. He built many churches in his attenuated Perpendicular style, of which the best examples are St. Michael's, Camden Town, London; St. Augustine's, Pendlebury, Manchester; St. Martin's, Scarborough; St. German's, Roath; and Holy Trinity, Kensington.

31   *Church of the Holy Redeemer, Clerkenwell, 1888, by J. D. Sedding*

Another high-churchman and friend of this group was J. D. Sedding, whose church [31] of the Holy Redeemer, Clerkenwell, London (1888), has a

Gothic counterpart in his famous church of Holy Trinity, Sloane Street. Scott, Bodley and Sedding go with plainsong, the English Hymnal, Percy Dearmer and the later phases of the Catholic Revival. Their buildings are set in slums, where the Church of England did such great work throughout the last half of the century, and in spacious seaside suburbs, whose wealthy and well-intentioned congregations subscribed to the slum missions.

32   *Design for a Church by Edgar Wood*

The Nonconformists were now tiring of their Classical chapels (see pp. 90–119) and taking to what was known as "late Gothic freely treated." Here is an example by Edgar Wood, who was born a Methodist [32].

Temple Moore, another of the older Scott's pupils, survived until 1920, and he built in a severe and simple late Gothic style, among the finest examples of which are St. Wilfrid's, Harrogate (1909) [33], and one of his latest works, Pusey House, Oxford. Sir Charles Nicholson and Harold Gibbons are architects in the Temple Moore tradition. With these men must be included Micklethwaite and Somers Clark and their pupil Harold S. Rogers. The Roman

33   *St. Wilfrid's, Harrogate, 1909, by Temple Moore*

Catholic architect of this date was J. F. Bentley whose Cathedral at Westminster [34] in the Basilican style (designed 1895) and church of the Holy
Rood at Watford in late Gothic are a testimony to the versatility of his great
genius.

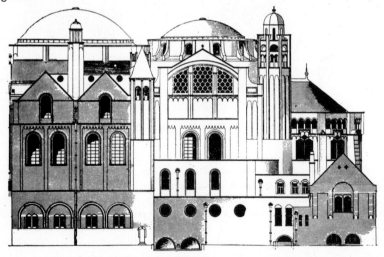

34   *Westminster Cathedral, designed 1895, by J. F. Bentley*

SOME CURIOUS REVIVALS. In Secular life there was now a restlessness among architects to find a manner of building which, in style at any rate, did not savour of either Gothic or classic. Influenced by Norman Shaw, Thomas G. Jackson, a fine writer on architecture, revived the Jacobean style for his

35 *Examination Schools, Oxford, 1876, by Thomas G. Jackson*

prize-winning design for the Examination Schools, Oxford [35], in 1876. He did so much else in this manner that it came to be known as Anglo-Jackson. The manufacturer of Holloway's Female Pills, wishing to educate women as well as make them well, sent W. H. Crossland, a pupil of Sir Gilbert Scott, to the French châteaux. As a result Crossland produced the amazing

Holloway College for Women (1886) at Egham [36] in Portland stone and red brick, vaster and more elaborate than Chambord and set among pines and rhododendrons of Surrey. That fine draughtsman and architect Beresford Pite won the Soane Medallion in 1882 with his design for "A West End Club House" [37] in what might be called a Wagnerian romantic style. He designed the West End to go with it.

36   *Royal Holloway College, Englefield Green, Surrey, finished 1886, by W. H. Crossland*

At the other end of the scale C. R. Mackintosh went in search of extreme simplicity and built in a Beardsleyesque Scottish Baronial style. This design of a house by him [38] is early-twentieth-century. With George Walton he was known by the followers of Norman Shaw as a member of the "Spook School" and he is really an Art Nouveau architect, a romantic, not a down-to-earth man like Voysey, Scott, Edgar Wood and Holden, whose Market Hall [39] of 1901 is a foretaste of the underground stations and the new University of London building, for which he is now known.

VICTORIAN SURVIVAL. The great church architect Sir Ninian Comper was a pupil of Bodley. His early work is mostly late Gothic, more gorgeously

37   *Design for "A West End Club House", by Beresford Pite, 1882*

38   *The Hill House, Helensburgh, 1906, by C. R. Mackintosh*

39   *Design for a Market Hall, 1901, by C. H. Holden*

treated in colour of glass, hangings and painted woodwork than was that of his master. St. Cyprian's, Clarence Gate, Baker Street, London, 1900 [40],

40   *St. Cyprian's, Baker Street, 1900, by Sir Ninian Comper*

is an example of his earlier style. He builds his churches as "a lantern for the altar" and intends them to bring the visitor, as he enters them, to his knees. He obtains his effects by plan, colour and above all a sure sense of proportion. St. Philip's, Cosham [41] is a 1937 building shewing his development and what might have been the development, had they survived, of the great Victorian church-builders. The altar is brought out into the middle of the church so that a congregation may join in worship from three sides. It is still the central flame of the lantern, under its golden baldachino. Classic and Gothic are welded together in the church itself. It is the end of the battle of Gothic and Classic, "inclusion by unity" as Comper calls it. The late A. Randall Wells, the late F. C. Eden and the late Martin Travers, who was a pupil of Comper, and T. Lawrence Dale, Frederick Etchells, F.R.I.B.A., and R. Blacking are among the stalwarts of this tradition of good craftsmanship.

41   *St. Philip's, Cosham, 1937, by Sir Ninian Comper*

13 THREE CHURCHES

BLISLAND, CORNWALL

CHURCH CRAWLING is the richest of pleasures, it leads you to the remotest and quietest country, it introduces you to the history of England in stone and wood and glass which is always truer than what you read in books. It was through looking at churches that I came to believe in the reason why churches were built and why, despite neglect and contempt, innovation and business bishops, they still survive and continue to grow and prosper, especially in our industrial towns.

Of all the country churches of the West I have seen I think the Church of St. Protus and St. Hyacinth, Elisland, in Cornwall, is the most beautiful. I was a boy when I first saw it, thirty or more years ago. I shall never forget that first visit—bicycling to the inland and unvisited parts of Cornwall from my home by the sea. The trees at home were few and thin, sliced and leaning away from the fierce Atlantic gales, the walls of the high Cornish hedges were made of slate stuffed in between with fern and stone crop and the pulpy green triangles of mesembreanthemum, sea vegetation of a windy sea coast country. On a morning after a storm, blown yellow spume from Atlantic rollers would be trembling in the wind on inland fields. Then, as huge hill followed huge hill and I sweated as I pushed my bicycle up and heart-in-mouth went swirling down into the next valley, the hedges became higher, the lanes ran down ravines, the plants seemed lusher, the thin Cornish elms seemed bigger and the slate houses and slate hedges gave place to granite ones. I was on the edge of Bodmin Moor, that sweet brown home of Celtic saints, that haunted, thrilling land so full of ghosts of ancient peoples whose hut circles, beehive dwellings and burial mounds jut out above the ling and heather. Great wooded valleys, white below the trees with wood anemones or blue with bluebells, form a border fence on this, the western side of Bodmin Moor.

Perched on the hill above the woods stands Blisland village. It has not one ugly building in it and, which is unusual in Cornwall, the houses are round a green. Between the lichen-crested trunks of elm and ash that grow on the green, you can see everywhere the beautiful moorland granite. It is used for windows, for chimney stacks, for walls. One old house has gable ends carved in it. They are sixteenth or seventeenth century and curl round like swiss rolls. The church is down a steep slope of graveyard, past slate headstones and it looks over the tree tops of a deep and elmy valley and away to the west where, like a silver shield, the Atlantic shines. An opening in the churchyard circle shows a fuchsia hedge and the Vicarage front door beyond. The tower is square and weathered and made of enormous blocks of this moorland granite, each block as big as a chest of drawers. When I first saw it, the tower was stuffed with moss and with plants which had rested here and there between the great stones. But lately it has been most vilely repointed in hard straight lines with cement. The church itself which seems to lean this way and that, throws out chapels and aisles in all directions. It hangs on the hillside, spotted with lichens which have even softened the slates of its roof. Granite forms the tracery of its windows, there is a granite holy-water stoup in the porch.

The whitewashed porch, the flapping notices, the door! That first thrill of turning the handle of the door of a church never seen before, or a church dearly loved and visited again and again like Blisland—who but the confirmed church crawler knows it?

Sir Ninian Comper, that great church architect, says that a church should bring you to your knees when first you enter it. Such a church is Blisland. For there before me as I open the door is the blue-grey granite arcade, that hardest of stones to carve. One column slopes outwards as though it was going to tumble down the hill and a carved wooden beam is fixed between it and the south wall to stop it falling. The floor is of blue slate and pale stone. Old carved benches of dark oak and a few chairs are the seating. The walls are white, the sun streams in through a clear west window and there—glory of glories! —right across the whole eastern end of the church is a richly-painted screen and rood loft. It is of wood. The panels at its base are red and green. Wooden columns, highly coloured and twisted like barley sugar, burst into gilded tracery and fountain out to hold a panelled loft. There are steps to reach this loft, in the wall. Our Lord and His Mother and St. John who form the rood are over the centre of the screen. I look up and there is the old Cornish roof, shaped like the inside of an upturned ship, all its ribs richly carved, the carving shown up by white plaster panels. Old roofs, beautifully restored, are to be seen throughout the church. They stretch away beyond the cross irregularly and down the aisles. I venture in a little further, there through this rich screen I mark the blazing gold of the altars and the medieval-style glass, some of the earliest work of Mr. Comper. In the nave is a pulpit shaped like a wineglass, in the Georgian style and encrusted with cherubs and fruit carved in wood.

The screen, the glory of the church, the golden altars, the stained glass and the pulpit are comparatively *new*, designed by F. C. Eden in 1897, who died a few years ago. He must have visualised this Cornish church as it was in medieval times. He did not do all the medieval things he might have done. He did not paint the walls with pictures of angels, saints and devils, he left the western windows clear that people might see their books; he put in a *Georgian* pulpit. He centred everything on the altar to which the screen is, as it were, a golden, red and green veil to the holiest mystery behind it.

What do dates and style matter in Blisland church? There is

Norman work in it and there is fifteenth- and sixteenth-century work and there is sensitive and beautiful modern work. But chiefly it is a living church whose beauty makes you gasp, whose silent peace brings you to your knees, even if you kneel on the hard stone and slate of the floor, worn smooth by generations of worshippers.

The valley below the church was hot and warm when first I saw this granite cool interior. Valerian sprouted on the Vicarage wall. A fig tree traced its leaves against a western window. Grasshoppers and birds chirruped. St. Protus and St. Hyacinth, patron saints of Blisland church, pray for me! Often in a bus or train I call to mind your lovely church, the stillness of that Cornish valley and the first really beautiful work of man which my boyhood vividly remembers.

MILDENHALL, WILTS

Ah let me enter, once again, the pew
Where the child nodded as the sermon grew;
Scene of soft slumbers! I remember now
The chiding finger; and the frowning brow
Of stern reprovers, when the ardent June
Flung through the glowing aisles the drowsy noon;
Till closed the learn'd harangue, with solemn look
Arose the chaunter of the sacred book—
The parish clerk (death-silenced) far-famed then
And justly, for his long and loud—Amen!
Rich was his tone, and his exulting eye
Glanced to the ready choir, enthroned on high,
Nor glanced in vain; the simple hearted throng
Lifted their voices, and dissolved in song;
Till in one tide, deep rolling, full and free
Rung through the echoing pile, old England's psalmody.[1]

In all England there are probably hardly more than a hundred churches which have survived the tampering of the last ninety years.

[1] From *My Native Village*, N. T. Carrington, 1830.

We talk of our churches as "old" but they are mainly Victorian—at any rate in their furniture. The West galleries were cut down. The old choir was dismissed and went disgruntled off to chapel or to form a village band or to appear self-consciously and surpliced in the chancel. That chancel was blocked by an organ or harmonium, its width was cluttered up with choirstalls, the pulpit was removed, the plaster taken off the walls, the ceiling stripped, the high pews chopped down, the clear windows filled with coloured glass, the old floor paved with red and shiny tiles. All the texture and atmosphere of the past were replaced by a sticky and glossy hardness which was wrongly, if piously, thought to be medieval.

Of all the churches which remain almost untouched by the Victorians, the loveliest I know is Mildenhall, near Marlborough. It stands in the Kennet water meadows, a simple four-square affair: three-storeyed tower, nave, aisles either side and a chancel. But as you approach it there are signs of the past—clear glass panes, patched and flaking outside walls looking like an old water colour. And then the inside! You walk into the church of a Jane Austen novel, into a forest of magnificent oak joinery, an ocean of box pews stretching shoulder high all over the church. Each is carved with decorations in a Strawberry Hill Gothick manner. The doors and sides of the pews take a graceful curve either side of the font and another curve above them is made by the elegant west gallery. Norman pillars just raise their sculptured heads above the woodwork of the aisles. Two huge pulpits stand, one each side of the chancel arch. The old stone floors remain, the long cream-washed walls, the stone arch mouldings, picked out subtly white to form a pale contrast. The chancel, as it should be, is richest of all—panelled, with elaborate-carved pews for the squarson and his family, a carved canopy hanging over the Commandment board behind the altar, delicately carved communion rails in the Chippendale style. Even the red leather kneelers at these rails and the scarlet service books are the same date—1816. For there it is, written in gold letters on shields that look down from the corbels of the nave roof:—

"This church deeply in decay has been all but rebuilded generously and piously at their own expense by—"

and then are given the names of the churchwardens and ten other men who loved their church.

It is not simply that it is an *old* building that makes this church so beautiful (there are thousands of old churches) it is that it contains all its Georgian fittings. Though the date is 1816, the style and quality of workmanship is that of fifty years earlier. I believe the designer was one of the Pinch family who must also have built the cross-shaped village school with its octagonal Gothick style tower in the centre and who designed Hungerford church and later did some churches and houses in Bath and the Isle of Man. Whoever he was, he was an artist.

Through the clear glass windows you can see the Kennet meadows, the brick and thatched cottages of the village and to the south the chalky-green cliff fringed by overhanging beeches of Savernake Forest. The Rector (a squarson) before this one preserved the eighteenth-century tradition I have seen nowhere else. He changed in the chancel and his scarf and surplice hung over the communion rails during the week. He used one pulpit for the service and crossed to the other for the sermon. Grand and reposeful those sermons were in the oil lamp-light (now alas, replaced by gas) as one sat penned up in a box pew and saw his fine eighteenth-century figure towering above one in the tall pulpit. He was a great man, loved in the neighbourhood and so no doubt is his successor, but I have never "sat under him" as the old-fashioned phrase of sermon-tasters goes.

Mildenhall is a patriarchal country church. It is the embodiment of the Church of England by law established, the still heart of England, as haunting to my memory as the tinkle of sheep bells on the Wiltshire

Downs. It puts me in mind of Jane Taylor's poem, 'The Squire's Pew':—

> *A slanting ray of evening light*
> *Shoots through the yellow pane;*
> *It makes the faded crimson bright,*
> *And gilds the fringe again:*
> *The window's gothic frame-work falls*
> *In oblique shadow on the walls.*
>
> *And since those trappings first were new,*
> *How many a cloudless day,*
> *To rob the velvet of its hue,*
> *Has come and passed away!*
> *How many a setting sun hath made*
> *That curious lattice-work of shade.*[1]

ST. MARK'S, SWINDON

How different is the atmosphere in the churches of Swindon. The train draws into the outskirts. One hundred and eight years ago, there was nothing here at all but a canal and a place where two newly-built railways joined, the Cheltenham and Great West Union Railway (the Gloucestershire line) and the London to Bristol line, known as the Great Western and which not rack or thumb screw will ever induce me to call *Western Region British Railways*. On a hill above the meadow was the old market town of Swindon. Then New Swindon was built in the meadow by the Great Western. It was a convenient point between Bristol and London. It consisted of sheds, and a few rows of model cottages with open fields round them. These cottages are of Bath stone taken from the excavations of Box Tunnel. They still exist and are called the Company's Houses. They must form one of the earliest-planned industrial estates in Britain.

The parishioners of St. Philip and St. Jacob in Bristol entreated the

[1] From *Essays in Rhyme on Morals and Manners* (London: Houlston & Co., 1840).

Great Western to build a church for their workers; directors stumped up money, subscriptions were raised, land was presented and by 1845, St. Mark's church was built.

There it stands today close beside the line on the Bristol side of the station. A stone building, all spikes and prickles outside, designed by Gilbert Scott who was then a young man and who lived to build hundreds of rather dull copy-book churches all over Britain, and to build St. Pancras Hotel, the Foreign Office in London and to restore many cathedrals.

One cannot call it a convenient site. Whistles and passing trains disturb the services, engine smoke blackens the leaves and tombstones, and eats into the carved stonework of the steeple. But it is a strong church and though it is not much to look at, it is for me the most loved church in England. For not carved stones nor screen and beautiful altars, nor lofty arcades nor gilded canopies, but the priests who minister and the people who worship make a church strong. If ever I feel England is pagan, and that the poor old Church of England is tottering to its grave, I revisit St. Mark's, Swindon. That corrects the impression at once. A simple and definite faith is taught; St. Mark's and its daughter churches are crowded. Swindon, so ugly to look at to the eyes of the architectural student, glows golden as the New Jerusalem to eyes that look beyond the brick and stone.

For there is no doubt that Swindon *is* superficially ugly. That pretty model village of the eighteen-forties has developed a red brick rash which stretches up the hill to Old Swindon and strangles it, and beyond Old Swindon it runs tentacles to the downs and it spreads with monotony in all other directions. It is now the biggest town in Wiltshire, sixty times the size of the original market town. But I would rather see a red brick rash like Swindon (for it has few, if any, slums) enlivened with Victorian towers and steeples sticking out of it, than I would see a gleaming glass city of architect-designed flats with never a church but instead only the humped backs of super-cinemas, the grand-stands of greyhound tracks and the bubbling cocoa fountains for the community workers.

Swindon is largely a Christian town and much of the credit for that goes to the priests and people of St. Mark's. It is not Sabbatarian and smug. It has its cinemas and theatres and art gallery and library and sports grounds and the Swindon Town Football Club—but the churches too are part of its life. That is its distinction.

In the Centenary book of St. Mark's which appeared in 1945, there is a photograph of Canon Ponsonby wearing side whiskers and a beard that ran under his chin but not over it. This saintly Victorian priest (who died in 1945 aged nearly 100), caused St. Mark's parish so to grow in faith that it built four other churches in New Swindon. One of them, St. Paul's, became a separate parish. He also caused the Wantage Sisters to open their mission house in Swindon. The work went on under the famous Canon Ross, his successor, and it continues. The most beautiful daughter church of St. Mark's was built, called St. Luke's. It was designed by W. A. Masters. Except for the railway works which are awe inspiring inside, St. Luke's is the only fine interior, architecturally, in Swindon. But it is not with lovely St. Luke's nor with little St. John's nor with the mission which St. Mark's supports abroad, nor with the many priests who have been Swindon men that I want to end. On the steep hill that winds from the old to the new Town there is a church built of wood called St. Saviour's. It was erected in 1889–90 in six months by St. Mark's men, mostly railway workers. They did this in their spare time and for nothing. Some of them sacrificed their holidays and their working hours were from 6.00 a.m. to 5.30 p.m. in those days. What faith must have inspired them to go out after a long day's work and build a church.

Of course, with foundations of Faith like this, St. Saviour's grew and in 1904 it had to be enlarged. Over a hundred men once again set to work and the church was extended entirely by voluntary labour and in spare time.

St. Mark's parish for some reason hangs together and is a living community, full of life and spirit. Perhaps it is because Swindon is the right size for an industrial town, neither too big nor too small. Perhaps it is because the sort of work men do in a railway works— "inside" as they call it in Swindon—is not soul-destroying such as one sees in motor factories where the ghastly chain belt system persists. Perhaps it is not beneath the dignity of men. Whatever it is, I know that the people of Swindon first taught me not to judge people by the houses they live in, nor churches only by their architecture. I would sooner be on my knees within the wooden walls of St. Saviour's than leaning elegantly forward in a cushioned pew in an Oxford College chapel—that is to say if I am to realise there is something beyond this world worth thinking about.

The church-crawler starts by liking *old* churches, but he ends by liking all churches and of all churches those that are most alive are often those hard-looking buildings founded by Victorian piety— churches like St. Mark's, Swindon.

14   COAST AND COUNTRY[1]

Ventnor

FAR too few people on the Isle of Wight have the sense to go by its railways. These delicious single lines wind through most of the best scenery of the island. Oh, let me advise you instead of sitting half-asleep in the luxury coach with your arm round your girl and the wireless on and the petrol pumps passing and the gear-clashing and brakes squeaking at dangerous corners—oh, let me advise you to go by train. And of all lines on the Isle of Wight, the fairest and wildest, the most countrified, the most romantic is that which runs from Cowes, not Ryde, to Ventnor West, not the main station of Ventnor.

It was by this line that I, almost the only passenger, first came to Ventnor. And if the Southern Railway had any sense it would put observation cars on this part of its system.

We glide through alder-bordered meadows, past the thatched farms and greeny-grey stone cottages of inland Wight. Little streams and meadow-sweet, Shorthorns and Friesians—an inland agricultural country that might not be an island at all; which is yet like neither Hants nor Dorset.

Then the chalky downs grow nearer, high and golden-brown with grass—the blackness of a tunnel—half a mile of it—and we are out in

[1] The following pieces were written for the wireless and were performed on the Western Region, the happiest of all broadcasting places. They were written to read aloud, a sort of prose lyric to convey the picture and atmosphere of a place. They passed the test of Mr. Rupert Annand their producer, who altered with unerring ear the awkward-sounding sentences.

the jungle of the Amazon, or so it seems. For here at St. Lawrence Halt and all along the sea coast to Ventnor West are strangled shrubs and luxurious undergrowth. Sycamores and ash trees wave above us and below us, old man's beard and bind-weed clamber over broken stone walls, damp-looking drives wind down to empty stables and huge houses turned into holiday camps are left to ghosts and centipedes, and all the time, between the ash tree branches, an unexpected silver, shines the sea.

Ventnor! Here we are at Ventnor West! Not a sign of a town. But most of Ventnor is a park. The shopping streets are tucked away in a hollow. There are more steps than there are roads, for the town climbs up-hill for 400 feet from the sea, and for 400 feet above the top of the town rises the wooded height of St. Boniface Down. Most towns are horizontal. Ventnor is perpendicular. It is all trees and steps and zig-zag roads and everywhere there are beautiful gardens, public and private.

Some thousands of years ago with a roar and a crunch or may be more slowly and less dramatically than that, six miles of these chalky cliffs eight-hundred feet high, subsided into the channel. But these six miles did not quite sink into the sea. What with streams and falling earth and nature, these fallen cliffs became a luxuriant land of their own. Today they are known as the Undercliff. Artists came to see them more than a century ago, when the sea and rocks and huge chasms were beginning to be appreciated. Many books were published with steel engravings of the Isle of Wight. The nobility and gentry built themselves marine villas of enormous size upon the Undercliff—cottages they called them but we would call them palaces. They bought their crabs and lobsters from the fishermen who lived in squalid cots beside the sand at Ventnor cove. Then Queen Victoria and Prince Albert came to live at Osborne so the Isle of Wight was all the rage and no place more the rage than Ventnor. Little Osbornes were built on every available piece of cliff, every ledge and cranny and each little Osborne had its garden of palms, myrtles and hydrangeas and its glimpse of sea.

And there they are today, unchanged. In the Parish Magazine of St. Catherine's (the Parish Church of the town) the Vicar pleads for more permanent residents. "There are many people anxious to make their homes in Ventnor," he says. And I, for the moment, am one of them; though I think St. Alban's up three hundred and fifty steps would be my place of worship, so long as my heart would stand it. In that mild air which is not heavy, how gladly would I live and die.

Of all seaside towns I have seen, Ventnor looks after its outward appearance best. The public gardens are amazing. The rockery around the sea front, is always a mass of flowers; orange, pink and purple seem to be the favourite colours. The Park is wild on the seaward side but on the land-ward leaning slopes it is red, white and blue with municipal gardening which suits so well this Victorian town.

The sudden valleys in Ventnor between one bit of cliff and the next are so hot and still and so full of flowers that one almost expects a bird of paradise to flit from prunus to prunus or an alligator to slither out from underneath a palm. And then in another hundred yards is open cliff and familiar chalky cliff flowers. Swinburne lies in Bonchurch graveyard here by Ventnor town. No one made the sea hiss and clang in English poetry better than he. The sea he sang keeps Ventnor fresh, for all its tropic vegetation. The sound of its waves on chalk and sand is never long out of your ears; the sound of the sea travels upwards in this amphitheatre of wooded and tremendous hills.

In and Around Freshwater, I.O.W.

The stone of the Isle of Wight; that is what impresses me most each time I visit it. The stones and sands of the Island seem brighter in colour even than the trees and flowers. And these rocks—bands of sand and half-rock are torn up into such shapes, such stripes and colours, such gorges or chines, that one feels that Western Wight is an earthquake poised in mid-explosion, and ready any day to burst its turfy covering of wild, distorted downs.

One goes to Freshwater via the Lymington Ferry to Yarmouth. The little town spreads out along this flat north coast at the mouth of its tidal river. Old red-tiled roofs contrast with silvery-white stone walls; ilex and seaside elms and firs form a dark background. Yarmouth is mostly a Georgian town, in brick and stone with a sixteenth-century church, uneven, rugged and beautiful.

One of the prettiest buildings in Yarmouth is a private house called "The Mount," built in the late eighteenth or early nineteenth century, of white bricks. Its beauty is all in its proportions—the relation of window to wall space, and the planted clumps of trees around it affording its owners a glimpse across the Solent to Hampshire and the New Forest. Most of the finest old houses and towns of Wight are inland, or along this uneventful north coast. The worship of the sea and nature in the raw is at its earliest a late-Georgian cult.

Newtown, near Yarmouth, once a town is now only an oyster fishery, and a few old cottages arranged in streets on an eminence in the salt marshes, with estuary all round. It sent two members to Parliament until 1832. The Town Hall remains, a Jacobean building, but where are the Mayor and Corporation? The market days and fair days? Ask of the sea-birds that sail above its vast, deserted stretch of harbour water. "Gone, gone," they cry. And Newtown is now one of the most romantic and, thank heaven, least visited places in all the Island.

Freshwater with its red brick villas is quite out of tune with the local styles and colours. Once, no doubt, it was lovely—a little straw-thatched village with cottages and church of honey-coloured stone on the most inland reach of the tidal river Yar. But there are still hilly lanes in it, and a few fields.

In its best days Tennyson knew it. His house at Farringford, now an hotel, is still the loveliest big house in Freshwater. It is a long, low

Georgian building in a sweet and fancy Gothic style of the period, a good deal older than Tennyson. It has its little park of elm and ilex, and its main views, as usual, away from the elements. It is an enlarged version of Somersby Rectory, Lincolnshire, where Tennyson was born. Even the scenery is somewhat similar, being chalk downland. But the sea, instead of lying beyond miles of Lincolnshire marsh and fen, is almost at your feet.

> *"Something betwixt a pasture and a park*
> *Saved from sea breezes by a hump of down"*

wrote Sir Henry Taylor, and that still describes Farringford; the hump of Down is High Down with Tennyson's monument on top of it, and white chalk cliff falling sheer for five hundred feet into the channel.

To walk along High Down towards the Needles is like a thrilling and terrifying dream. Behind stretches the coast of Wight to St. Catherine's Point, a series of changing effects from this whitest of white chalk (white paper or linen look cream-coloured beside it), to the pink and honey and gold and grey of the points behind us. Probably this south-western coast of Wight is the longest stretch of unspoiled and colossal landscape in the south-west of England. The few houses visible along it are old thatched farms in hollows of the downs. Not even the convoys of luxury coaches bowling along the coast road take the remoteness from these stupendous stretches of coloured and distorted rock. And here ahead are the Needles. The turf narrows, till suddenly you are aware that there is sea on either side of you, milky-green four hundred feet below, and the Needle rocks themselves glitter and lean sideways out of the sea. Then just when the point might have narrowed to but a razor's edge of turf, there is a fence so that you have to turn back. And this is the time, if it is afternoon, to take a look at Alum Bay which is on the Solent side of the Needles. I came to it first the usual coach way, parking where the ice cream kiosks stand among the gorse bushes, came from the villa-dom of Totland which is like Bromley or Muswell Hill set down by the sea.

Alum Bay is a well-known "beauty spot," and I suspect such places. But of all "beauty spots" I have seen, Alum Bay is the most certainly entitled to be called beautiful. An L-shaped bay—the long part of the L a pearly height of chalk cliff 400 feet high, stretching out into the sea, no sand below it and the great merciless cliffs of chalk glittering brighter as the sun moves round to the west. And here above a shingly shore is a series of promontories not quite so high as the chalk. Walk along the shingle to the arm of chalk, and then look back at these capes. One is brilliant gold; the next is white; the next purple; the next grey; the next black with streaks of green. In great broad bands these strips of colour run down the cliffs, turning the sky pale with the richness of their colour. "Alum Bay; one side of it a wall of glowing chalk, and the other a barrier of rainbows," says my good Victorian guide book, and it does not exaggerate.

I am torn in mind between the three great beauties of Western Wight: the silvery-green inland country along the railway line from Yarmouth to Newport with its glimpses of old stone manor farms, thatched cottages and protecting hump of Downs, Dorset without the flint; the colossal untamed landscape of the south-west coast from the Needles to St. Catherine's point, and Alum Bay. They are all beautiful and all can be seen from Freshwater.

Hayling Island

> *Hayling Island!   Hayling Island!*
> *What did I expect to see?*
> *Beetling cliff and chalky highland,*
> *And the salt spray splashing me?*

But this was quite the wrong picture. If it was not for the long wooden toll bridge from Havant—a halfpenny for foot passengers, 8d. for motor cars—or the short, choppy ferry from Portsmouth, you would never know you were on an island at all. The Hayling people certainly must always remember they are islanders, for if ever they wish to go shopping, or out to tea in some place that is not Hayling, they must pay toll or ferry fare.

Hayling is just a piece of inland Hampshire that has slithered—oaks, elms, winding lanes and all—out of England into the sea. As for beetling cliffs and chalky highlands, they are not to be seen, the twelve square miles of the place are flat as a pancake. As for salt spray splashing me, even the open bit of coast at the southern end is rarely troubled by great waves, for the Isle of Wight and Selsey Bill protect Hayling from any big seas that come charging in from the English Channel.

The island is like the letter T lying upside down in salt water, the cross beam of the T facing the open water. Along the four and a half miles of this cross beam is a stretch of windy beach with a great deal of fine greyish-silver sand. Then the long narrow upright part of this inverted letter stretches north towards the mainland. Either side of it are the vast and lake-like reaches of Chichester Harbour on the east with the flat Sussex coast in view; Langstone Harbour on the west with the smoke, gasworks, cranes and chimneys of Portsmouth uncompromisingly present. Far inland is the noble outline of Portsdown.

There is no doubt that the way to see Hayling is on a bicycle or on foot. "It's so beautiful here in May and June," a postman said to me, "that I often feel I should pay for bicycling about these flowery lanes instead of being paid to do it." And the pleasure of the island is partly the sudden sight of salt water.

I walked down a narrow lane, past bungalows drowned in flowering shrubs, past hedges and under elms. Then I found a path bordered with long grass topped with cow parsley, so that the effect was of breaking rollers rearing backwards to leave me a walking space; and then suddenly there was a pebbly strand with calm harbour water stretching for miles, with sailing boats and dinghies dotting the middle distance, and inland oaks and ilex hanging over the salt waters, and not a soul in sight. And there was the ripple and suck of a smooth tide flooding over silvery mud and the salt, sand-coated vegetation of the marshes. That is part of the quiet country Hayling—the oldest Hayling.

The island divides itself into three kinds of life—farming, amateur sailing, and seaside holiday camps. But the oldest, the farming life, is obviously most efficient. The land is rich; gardens, golden melancholy Guernseys browsing in meadows of clover, rich flat fields on the west and north all proclaim that. Right in the middle by the shops, near the red-brick cinema and the bus stops, is a big thatched dairy farm, where Guernseys look sadly out of their stalls at passing motor buses and motor cars. "Rus in urbe," indeed.

The two old country churches are founded in agriculture. They are stone buildings of about 1150, each with central tower, shingled spire and lean-to aisles. The smaller one at North Hayling is the prettier, with its sloping east wall buttressed up from falling into the road, and its old timbered roofs and porches, for it has been less tinkered with by the Victorians than the other.

Here and there in the Island old brick cottages with thatched roofs remind one of the country quiet. But what, I ask myself, can account for these trim houses hidden among wind-slashed oaks and elms, each with its mown lawn and quota of purple aubretia, its flowering prunus and scarlet-flowered japonica? The answer is not far to seek. In sheltered creeks on the coast of Hayling are moored privately-owned yachts and dinghies. The directory shows me that captains in the Royal Navy, and even admirals, inhabit the houses around. Colonels too, at last able to indulge their taste for sailing, find retirement here from Army life. Bronzed men in shorts or corduroys with open shirts instead of the dazzling uniforms of their regular occupations are messing about here in boats. The flap of sail, the creak of rowlocks, the splash of water bailed out of the hold, echo in each calm inlet.

I was down by a saltern at six o'clock—that magic hour when tackle is stowed and rubber-soled feet walk homeward from the quay. Cars drawn up outside one of those pretty sheltered houses told me that cocktail time had started. Here was the close and friendly fellowship of sailors—amateur and professional—those other permanent residents of the island besides farmers and tradesmen; contented and busy from one Regatta to another.

Lastly, there is the seaside life. This is seasonable. There is nothing so sad-looking as an amusement park which is not working. The Dodgems and the Giant Wheel down by the seashore rise inertly, among gorse and cupressus.

Some fields were full of empty caravans, the iron tables and chairs of tea places stood vacant in little gardens: no queues were at the ice cream kiosk which had just opened; no cars were parked along the shore. Winter salt had not yet been cleaned off the plate-glass windows of sun lounges in big hotels. Yet the only imposing architecture of Hayling Island—far more imposing than the two old churches or the cottages—is the gracious seaside architecture of another age which may be seen here at the Portsmouth end of the island. A stately Georgian crescent, worthy of Brighton itself, but unfinished, two large stucco Georgian houses near it, and some Italian-style villas behind, show that Hayling Island has been loved for its sands for more than a century.

In June the amusement park will be beginning to turn, families in bright summer clothes will be crowding into caravans, clubs and heads will be showing above the sand dunes of the golf course, bicycles will be stacked against walls, young limbs will be turning bronzed or freckled, stretched out on the long grey sands, shrimping nets and tin buckets will hang like fruit outside the shops. The seaside will be coming to life. From our villages the Mothers' Union or the Women's Institute will be packing into a coach for Hayling Island. They will cling to the sea front. In quieter reaches admirals, captains and colonels will be hoisting sail, and in elm and oak-protected fields farmers will be making hay while the sun shines—and so will everyone else.

Lyndhurst

Lyndhurst! Lyndhurst Way, Lyndhurst Grove, Lyndhurst Drive, Lyndhurst Crescent. The suburbs of England are full of the name. I cannot think why so small a place should so have taken the public fancy.

I believe Lyndhurst means "Forest of lime trees," but a more truthful description would be "Forest of Douglas firs" or even "Forest of oak and beech." Lyndhurst is the capital of the New Forest and it is up at the northern and wildest end, where Rufus was killed by an arrow.

The original New Forest, the Norman Forest, was of oak, then there were plantations of beech and later, in Victorian times, miles and miles of fir. People say you cannot properly see the New Forest from the main roads and they are quite right. But on a warm evening you can smell it between the wafts of petrol scent which linger on the tarmac— the resin scent among the conifers, the coconut smell of gorse on an open heath, the tropic scent like the Palm House at Kew under oaks and beeches, where holly shines and bracken is a young green.

Outside Lyndhurst the forest begins to look less wild. Victorian brick cottages peep about among the trees. Lodge gates stand guard to winding drives of laurel and azalea, at the end of which—how deep, how far, who knows?—are the country houses of the formerly rich. Five or six times a year perhaps, the verderers come to the Swainmote which is held in the King's House at Lyndhurst. Strange rights of turbary, pannage and smoke money go with certain old freehold cottages. The Forest laws are administered from Lyndhurst and it is as well to know some of them. For instance, an entomologist must apply to the King's House at Lyndhurst for a permit to catch moths and butterflies; and he is not allowed to sugar the trees. No licence is required, on the other hand, to be stung by flies among the oaks of the New Forest. These flies, called stouts, seem to carry small poisoned swords and draw blood. Hornets abound. When Tennyson, his wife and children and William Allingham, the poet, were swimming through bracken on July 15th, 1866, on their way to the great beeches of Mark Ash, Tennyson paused midway and said solemnly: "I believe this place is quite full of vipers." After going a little further he stopped again and said: "I am told that a viper bite may make a woman silly for life or deprive a man of his virility."

Despite the main roads and the modern houses and the coaches of Lyndhurst, wild life comes right into it. Wild New Forest ponies wait about outside the National Provincial Bank, or stand at the cross roads, in the middle of the traffic.

Lyndhurst is like Aldershot without the Army. Most of the houses are two storeys and the only old and remarkable one is the gabled King's House near the church. But before motor cars came into existence and with them the "caffs," "kiosks," guest-houses, before the petrol pumps, wires, poles and signs that follow the motor car— before all these things, Lyndhurst, lost in the Forest and its nearest railway station three miles away, must have been a paradise to stay in. Now it is a suburb for Southampton business people, with cricket grounds around it and a golf course.

Fifty years ago, artists, poets and musicians booked lodgings in the district. The huge Crown Hotel, rebuilt in 1897 in a half-timbered style, opposite the church, is a relic of those times. In fact Lyndhurst was the home of Victorian romance—wild nature after the smoke of towns, fir trees with a faintly Rhineland look, oak woods which took one back to the Forest of Arden, cultivated people instead of the vulgar throng. Ah! What a paradise it must have been to those rare Victorian souls! They expressed their gratitude in the huge church they built of red and yellow brick. Lyndhurst parish church was designed by William White and is in the most fanciful, fantastic Gothic style that ever I have seen, and I have seen a great deal. The spire itself is of brick, a remarkable feat. Inside, the brick columns have pipes of Purbeck round them and their capitals were carved by Mr Seale with leaves of New Forest trees. Unexpected dormers and gables jut out from the huge roof. The tracery of the windows is as strange as tropic plants. Some of the stained glass windows are by Morris and Burne-Jones and Rossetti. The prevailing colours inside are red and yellow. But Victorian stained glass and Victorian-coloured brick does *not* go with frescoes. Lord Leighton came to stay with Hamilton Aidé the song-writer and he painted a fresco over the altar of the church free of charge. It shows our Lord in white in the middle with the foolish virgins on one side and the wise ones on the other.

Lyndhurst church is capital, full of originality and thought and care. It expresses the courage and conviction of the Victorians. It is their lasting monument, towering on its mound above the gables of the Victorian houses and the oaks and beeches and fir trees of the New Forest.

Weymouth

Safe and wide and sheltered Weymouth Bay! Of course it is called the Naples of Dorset. But any seaside place whose bay is in the shape of a crescent is called the Naples of wherever it happens to be. The test is, is Naples called the Weymouth of Italy? No. When wet south-westerly gales such as Naples never saw are thundering on Chesil bank to the west of the town, when there is a smack and suck and roar of waves upon those miles of squeaking pebbles, so loud in its rolling of millions upon millions of sea-smoothed stones that the noise travels miles inland, then Weymouth lies snug and sheltered. That eerie Chesil Bank and the shelfed and lumpy length of Portland protect the place from the prevailing storms. The distant chalk and grassy downs of Dorset, studded with earthworks and tumuli, keep off the winds from the north. Though plumes of spray try to mount the cliff top, along all that white and shadowy stretch of splendour to the east of Weymouth—Durdle Door, Lulworth, and the Kimmeridge ledges to St. Alban's Head—Weymouth has no cliffs at all, unless you call its modest Georgian terraces and hotels cliffs. And spray does not often blow in at their windows.

Weymouth is on the mouth of the River Wey. It has water almost all round it—the brackish semi-tidal stretch of what once was called "the Backwater" behind the seaside part of the town. It is now known as "Radipole Lake" since Municipal effort is trying to develop it as an "amenity"—too late, I fear, for the railway runs close beside it and the new industrial suburb of Westham gives it a red brick crown. Salt marsh, unsuitable even for the greediest speculative builder as a site for seaside chalets, lies to the east of Weymouth. The River Wey runs out between old wharves and houses of the united towns of Weymouth and Melcombe Regis. And here the river is deep enough to harbour Channel Island steamers. If it were not for the gracious Georgian terraces, mostly of dark-red brick, relieved by bow windows, or by houses in silver-grey Portland stone, Weymouth would be, as it once was, two tiny villages either side of a tidal river, with acres of salt marsh and a wonderful sandy beach.

As it is, there are three Weymouths. The Weymouth of the Fleet, Weymouth itself, and Weymouth of the summer visitors.

Weymouth of the Fleet! From distant windy downs above the town, or better still, from that neck of railway, road and pebbles which links Portland to the mainland, may be seen in Portland harbour the ships of the Royal Navy, and lovely they look in the sunlight in their new greeny-grey coats of paint. And loveliest of all is the harbour, at night when the Fleet is in. Then not all the fairy lights and flood lights along the seafront of Weymouth round the corner could match this rival constellation to the heavens, twinkling against the velvet blackness of Portland. Ah, with what longing did the girls of Weymouth, Wyke and Rodwell, lean from upstairs windows and look across to those twinkling lights and whisper the magic words "The Fleet is in!" What dances! What parties! I once fell desperately in love with a Weymouth girl, the most beautiful girl I had ever seen in my life. I never declared my affection. I do not think I even had a dance with her. I just looked and loved while the moon shimmered in Weymouth Bay and the Fleet twinkled in Portland Harbour, and the band played *My Sweet Hortense*.

Now for Weymouth itself. It is Hardy's "Havenpool Town" where the Chapel Organist of his strange poem was seen by a suspicious member of the congregation "comrading close a sea-captain," it is old Weymouth. A place of narrow straight streets, still undisfigured. Every house that can has a bow window as though desperate to glimpse somehow the sky and the sea. The houses are mostly brick, a few stucco-faced. The graceful late Georgian bows are semicircular and rise to the first floor but do not generally reach the second floor. The bows are painted cream and their wooden cornices are well moulded. A few dignified classic buildings are in Portland stone—and how richly silvery-white this stone is here—where it is near its native quarry and unblackened by London smoke. The Guildhall, a stately building of 1836, in Greek Ionic style, and Melcombe Regis Parish Church are of this stone.

And what of Weymouth of the summer visitors? When George III stepped out of his bathing machine into the sea at Melcombe and the band struck up "God Save the King," he set a fashion. Then the town expanded in dark brick or silver stone terraces along the sea front. These terraces may not be grand Georgian like Brighton, but they are simple country work, a setting down by the sea of the decent houses of the county town of Dorchester. The best work of art in Weymouth (except possibly the forbidden Thornhill altar piece) is the statue of King George III where all the buses meet at the front. Poor good

King George who made Weymouth a famous watering place! What has Weymouth done to you but paint your statue and its attendant lions in garish colours, making you clash ridiculously with the noble Portland stone plinth on which you stand?

The sands and the bands and the bathing and the climate are all fine. But to see Georgian Weymouth going jazzy, to see arcades of pin-tables, blaring with electric lights and synthetic music, while the sun shines and the waves sparkle outside, to see hideous new buildings in white tiles jammed up against old brick and Portland stone, is rather like seeing an old woman in a dress too young for her. If Weymouth thinks the old woman is worth preserving, let her save the famous stretch of Georgian seafront, from the gentle beauty of Pultney and Devonshire Buildings at the west to the grander terraces on the east of the Esplanade. And let her save those modest Georgian streets and lanes of the old town. It will pay in the end. Buildings are the only record of civilisation. Weymouth still looks civilised. But how long will it be allowed to keep this asset of a civilised appearance?

Sidmouth

A silver mist of heat hung over Sidmouth when I came into it. A silver mist of heat was over it when I went away. The climate is so dominant in Sidmouth you can almost touch it. In Connaught Gardens—a modern piece of Italian-style gardening on a cliff top, with a view through arches of red cliffs five hundred feet high—sheltered from the sea breeze, plants would flower and flower as high as the cliffs themselves if only the wind would let them. For that is one of the first things I noticed about Sidmouth. As soon as I was out of the gentle sea breeze I was in a hot-house where wonderful west country bushes filled the air with scent, and enormous butterflies lit on asters and on antirrhinums, themselves twice as large as life. Fuchsia bells seemed three times the size of those anywhere else in Britain. If it were not for the sea Sidmouth, I thought, would be tropic forest. Devon hills protect it on all but the seaward side. Peakhill and Salcombe Hill guard the town west and east. Woods and little Devon fields climb their slopes. Other hills, blue-wooded, rise far inland. And here is the little valley of the River Sid—a brown moorland stream which disappears in shingle by the site of the old gasworks (now a car park) at one end of the sea front.

And on a piece of level ground saved from inundation by a pebble beach stands Sidmouth. Wooded glens rise inland. Huge cliffs, shaved down almost sheer, stretch pinkly to the east until they change to the white chalk of the Dorset coast. Westwards to Devon there is a mile-long beach below Peakhill where at low tide the stretch of sand changes from pink to gold as it goes further west. I could say that of all the seaside resorts I have seen on this tour, Sidmouth has the best sea from the children's point of view. That pebble beach is only a high tide affair. At low tide there is accommodation west of the town for all the population of Devon to play rounders by the salt sea waves. And ah! to bathe as I did in warm summer water, and swim towards the great pink cliffs and creamy stucco esplanade!

Despite these ample sands and hot-house garden walks, there are few chars-à-bancs. The crowds are neither vast nor noisy. No giant wheels nor kursaals intrude, no pier takes iron strides into the sea. The roads to Sidmouth are twisty, and the streets of the town are far too narrow even for private motors to move with ease, let alone chars-à-bancs. Sidmouth is indeed an exclusive place. It excludes the vulgar throng. No hideous jazz chain-stores, nor gimcrack concrete cages defile the quaintness of its older quarters.

The town is mostly Georgian with few newer additions than those put up in King Edward's reign. The style of the newest Sidmouth is a sort of red-brick Devonian baroque with green copper domes, and several humble terraces of yellow and red brick near the gasworks. The older and more gracious Sidmouth is Devonian too—low, two-storied stucco villas with green ironwork verandahs, some with pointed windows; some houses are Greek, little Parthenons among ilex trees, with hydrangeas by their front doors. Devon Georgian is the simplest, gayest, lightest, creamiest Georgian of all. I doubt if anywhere on the south coast there is a prettier Georgian stucco crescent than Fortfield Terrace which overlooks the cricket ground and sea, nor a more romantic fairy-tale-Gothic seaside house than Royal Glen a few hundred yards away. And round the Parish Church of St. Nicholas (mediæval and fairly high), and the newer Church of All Saints (Victorian and very low) are many stuccoed and barge-boarded villas, and beyond them villas of a latter age, Bournemouth in style, and many rare trees, wide gardens, flowering shrubs and carefully concealed tennis courts.

What a place to live in in the winter! Those old people I saw in the shops were clearly living on in a calm and civilised world which still lingers throughout the year in this equable climate. How they or anyone else have the money to keep up those big villas among the wooded glens, I do not know. Perhaps great sacrifices are made. If it is so I am glad it is, for they make Sidmouth civilised. What I am certain of is that in summer it is the hotel life that counts in Sidmouth. It is a town of vast hotels. From our table in the dining room, I saw beautiful button-nosed blondes who smiled secretly at young men in club blazers at neighbouring tables. Tennis-girl queens of Sidmouth! What romances must have started over coffee in basket chairs in the lounge, or on the hotel court during a strenuous single! What last walks there must have been at the end of the holidays, while in one of the glittering hotels in the valley below, parents are trying to like one another over a rubber of bridge. Sidmouth! silvery pink and creamy Sidmouth! Farewell!

Looe

I came to Looe by unimportant lanes. No main roads for me. I used a one-inch map. No hill was too steep, no village too remote or too full of witches. Thus I was able to taste the full flavour of the inland country behind Looe. Burnt brown August hedges were high as houses either side of narrow lanes. Grey-slated farms with granite round their windows hung on hill slopes. Little fields descended in steps of grass to deserted mines, to meadows heavy with the smell of mint.

On the hills above the lushness it is bleak indeed. Anything that dares to grow to any size is blown backwards from the sea. Ash trees and sloe bushes form a tunnel of twisted branches across the lane. Woods of oak and elm and beech belonging to mysterious country houses just peep above the hills and—phew!—the gale catches them, turns their leaves brown with salt and slices the tree-tops level with the hill.

Then, down, down, down for nearly two miles into Looe. I had a glimpse through oak trees of dark green river-water flecked with white wings of gulls. I saw overhanging woods enfolding the Looe and West Looe rivers, and in the mud the rotting hulks of ships.

Looe is two towns, East Looe and West Looe, one on each side of a steep valley. The oldest parts of the two towns are down on the waterside. Yachts, dinghies, and fishing boats are anchored in the river. There are wharves. They have old roofs of wonderful silvery-grey slate, and so have the older houses behind them. In East Looe, the bigger and more prosperous of the two old towns, the old streets are along the quay-sides. In West Looe the prettier and less-visited town, old houses climb a hill from an octagonal market house (1853), now a grocer's shop. The pavements on this hill are made of big brown pebbles; on either side of the road are white-washed cottages, black-tarred at their bases. It is quite easy to see how these two places grew, just from looking at the villages. And the best way to see them is not by road, but by water.

When I first came into Looe by road I was disappointed. I could hardly see the two old towns, and the long Victorian stone bridge which joins them—I could hardly see the houses for motor cars. Motor coaches from Manchester, new private cars like sleek sausages (priority for Government officials), battered pre-war motors belonging to failed literary gents like me, there they stretched along the quays in thousands. Wherever there was a space in either Looe for a car park there *was* a car park. And it was full. You could hardly hear the wail of seagulls above the dance music relayed from wireless sets in the new motor cars. Wasps gnawed at synthetic cakes in cafés. The fizzy lemonade that we drank with our fish and chips was warm. We could hardly move in the quaint old main streets of East Looe, for the thousands gazing into windows of Ye Olde Gifte Shoppes; chain stores jammed their flashy fronts into old houses. No guide books to Looe were available in any of the shops. And where, oh where was the sea? But the way to see the towns is by water.

As I put out the noise fell away. There were just the chug-chug of an outboard engine, the wail of gulls, the old and silvery wharves of Looe slipping past us as we headed up-stream for Trenant woods and those great lakes of dark green water I had seen as we entered the town. It is easy to see how the towns grew. First the ancient fishing ports either side of the water. They had their Mayors and Corporations, and sent Members to Parliament—the old rotten borough of pre-progressive days; birth-places of famous sailors, brave Elizabethans. Then a few Georgian houses were built inland, among these great enfolding woods where the two rivers divide and wind to nothingness deep in inland Cornwall. Then came the railway down the valley from Liskeard, in the wake of the new town hall and the ugly Victorian church of East Looe—the old parish church of St. Martin's, a splendid building, is more than a mile away up among the hills—and the town had started to change from fishing port to watering place. We turned the boat round and slid fast with the tide back along the quays. All up the cliffs above the town were perched the boarding houses,

Plymouth-style in grey cement or cream, drain pipes and bay window frames painted green, the name of the boarding house writ large on a board above the second floor windows. Most houses have a view above the old towns and out to cliffs and open sea. And here we were sliding past the Banjo pier and the tiny sand beach behind it, and out to open sea ourselves. We went round Looe island with its three houses and woodland belt of elder bushes. We saw the sloping cliffs by Talland church. We saw the cliffs stretch east to Downderry and Rame. They are not the great rocky heights of the north coast. They are greener, earthier, more sloping cliffs—but equally impressive. Looe was out of sight behind its headlands. Only modern bunga-lows beyond West Looe—with those detestable red roofs which look so ugly in the slate and granite of old Cornwall—only the bungalows remind us that we are not back in the ancient marine kingdom of Cornwall.

St. Endellion

Saint Endellion! Saint Endellion! The name is like a ring of bells. I travelled late one summer evening to Cornwall in a motor car. The road was growing familiar, Delabole with its slate quarry passed, then Pendogget. Gateways in the high fern-stuffed hedges showed sudden glimpses of the sea. Port Isaac Bay with its sweep of shadowy cliffs stretched all along to Tintagel. The wrinkled Atlantic Ocean had the evening light upon it. The stone and granite manor house of Tresungers with its tower and battlements was tucked away out of the wind on the slope of a valley and there on the top of the hill was the old church of St. Endellion. It looked, and still looks, just like a hare. The ears are the pinnacles of the tower and the rest of the hare, the church, crouches among wind-slashed firs.

On that evening the light bells with their sweet tone were being rung for practice. There's a Ringer's rhyme in the tower, painted on a board. It shows Georgian ringers in knee breeches and underneath is written a rhyme which ends with these fine four lines:

> *Let's all in love and Friendship hither come*
> *Whilst the shrill treble calls to thundering Tom*
> *And since bells are for modest recreation*
> *Let's rise and ring and fall to admiration.*

They were ringing rounds on all six bells. But as we drew near the tower—a grand, granite, fifteenth-century tower looking across half Cornwall—as we climed the hill the bells sounded louder even than the car. "St. Endellion! St. Endellion!" they seemed to say. "St. Endellion" their music was scattered from the rough lichened openings over foxgloves, over grey slate roofs, lonely farms and feathery tamarisks, down to that cluster of whitewashed houses known as Trelights, the only village in the parish, and to Roscarrock and Trehaverock and Trefreock, heard perhaps, if the wind was right, where lanes run steep and narrow to that ruined, forgotten fishing place of Port Quin, "St. Endellion!". It was a welcome to Cornwall and in front of us the sun was setting over Gulland and making the Atlantic at Polzeath and Pentire glow like a copper shield.

Ora pro nobis Sancta Endelienta! The words are carved in strangely effective lettering on two of the new oak benches in the church. Incidentally, those carved benches, which incorporate some of the old Tudor ones, are very decent-looking for modern pews. They were designed by the present rector and carved by a local sculptress. But who was St. Endellion? She was a sixth-century Celtic saint, daughter of a Welsh king, who with her sisters Minver and Teath and many other holy relations came to North Cornwall with the Gospel.

There was an Elizabethan writer who lived in the parish, Nicholas Roscarrock. He loved the old religion and was imprisoned in the Tower and put on the rack and then imprisoned again. He wrote the life of his parish saint. "St. Endelient" he called her and said she lived only on the milk of a cow: "which cowe the lord of Trenteny kild as she strayed into his grounds; and as olde people speaking by tradition, doe report, she had a great man to her godfather, which they also say was King Arthure, whoe took the killing of the cowe in such sort, as he killed or caus'd the Man to be slaine, whom she miraculously revived." Nicholas Roscarrock also wrote a hymn in her praise:

> *To emitate in part thy vertues rare*
> *Thy Faith, Hope, Charitie, thy humble mynde,*
> *Thy chasteness, meekness, and thy dyet spare*
> *And that which in this Worlde is hard to finde*
> *The love which thou to enemye didst showe*
> *Reviving him who sought thy overthrowe.*

When she was dying Endelient asked her friends to lay her dead body on a sledge and to bury her where certain young Scots bullocks or calves of a year old should of their own accord draw her. This they did and the Scots bullocks drew the body up to the windy hilltop where the church now stands.

The churchyard is a forest of upright Delabole slate headstones, a rich grey-blue stone, inscribed with epitaphs—the art of engraving lettering on slate continued in this district into the present century—names and rhymes set out on the stone spaciously, letters delicate and beautiful. From the outside it's the usual Cornish church—a long low building of elvan stone, most of it built in Tudor times. But the tower is extra special. It is of huge blocks of granite brought, they say, from Lundy Island. The ground stage of the tower is strongly moulded but the builders seem to have grown tired and to have taken less trouble with the detail higher up, though the blocks of granite are still enormous.

I can remember Endellion before its present restoration. There's a photograph of what it used to look like in the porch—pitchpine pews, pitchpine pulpit, swamping with their yellow shine the clustered granite columns of the aisles. Be careful as you open the door not to fall over.

Three steps *down* and there it is, long and wide and light and simple with no pitchpine anywhere except a lectern. A nave and two aisles with barrel roofs carved with bosses, some of them old but most of them done twelve years ago by a local joiner, the village postman and the sculptress. The floor is slate. The walls are stone lightly plastered blueish-grey. There is no stained glass. Old oak and new oak benches, strong and firm and simple, fill, but do not crowd, the church. They do not hide the full length of these granite columns. The high altar is long and vast. At the end of the south aisle is the sculptured base of St. Endelienta's shrine, in a blue-black slate called Cataclewse, a boxwood among stones. The church reveals itself at once. Though at first glance it is unmysterious, its mystery grows. It is the mystery of satisfying proportion—and no, not just that, nor yet the feeling of age, for the present church is almost wholly early Tudor, not very old as churches go, nor is the loving use of local materials all to do with it. Why does St. Endellion seem to go on praying when there is no one in it? The Blessed Sacrament is not reserved here, yet the building is alive.

There is something strange and exalting about this windy Cornish hill top looking over miles of distant cliffs, that cannot be put into words.

Down a path from the North door, bordered with fuchsias, is the Rectory. The Rector of St. Endellion is also a Prebendary. This church is run by a college of priests like St. George's Chapel, Windsor. There are four prebends in the college, though their building is gone and they live elsewhere. They are the prebends of Marny, Trehaverock, Endellion and Bodmin. Each of the Prebendal stalls has a little income attached to it and is held by local priests. The money is given to Christian causes. For instance, the Parish of Port Isaac, formed out of St. Endellion in 1913, is financed with the income of the Bodmin Prebendary. How this heavenly medieval arrangement of a college of prebendary clergymen survived the Reformation and

Commonwealth and Victorian interferers is another mystery of St. Endellion for which we must thank God. It was certainly saved from extinction by the late Athelstan Riley and Lord Clifden. Episcopal attacks have been made on it; but long live St. Endellion, Trehaverock, Marny and Bodmin! Hold fast. *Sancta Endelienta, ora pro nobis!*

The Rectors of St. Endellion have long been remarkable men. There was Parson Hocken, a blacksmith's son from St. Teath, who grew roses, was a Tractarian of the Parson Hawker type and when jeered at for his lowly origin hung a blacksmith's shoe over his pulpit and preached about it. There was Parson Josa, whom I just remember, who started as a choirboy in St. Peter's, Rome, and then joined our own Church of England; there is the present Rector, Prebendary Murphy, a joiner and scientist, and above all, a sound theologian. I can safely say, as an experienced sermon-taster of over forty summers, that he is the most interesting and sensible preacher I have heard. But sermons are not everything as all the rectors of St. Endellion have known.

I take a last look at St. Endellion standing on a cliff top of this Atlantic coast. The sun turns the water into moving green. In November weather, if the day is bright, the cliffs here are in shadow. The sun cannot rise high enough to strike them. The bracken is dead and brown, the grassy cliff tops vivid green; red berries glow in bushes. Ice cream cartons and cigarette packets left by summer visitors have been blown into crevices and soaked to pulp. The visitors are there for a season. Man's life on earth will last for seventy years perhaps. But this sea will go on swirling against these green and purple rocks for centuries. Long after we are dead it will rush up in waterfalls of whiteness that seem to hang half-way up the cliff face and then come pouring down with tons of ginger-beery foam. Yet compared with the age of these rocks, the sea's life is nothing. And even the age of rocks is nothing compared with the eternal life of man. And up there on the hill in St. Endellion church, eternal man comes week by week in the

Eucharist. That is the supreme mystery of all the mysteries of St. Endellion.

Port Isaac

Can it really be that a town is half a mile away? I have walked between high Cornish hedges from St. Endellion, once the parish church of Port Isaac. The tower dwindles. The lane winds. The slate of the hedges is overgrown with grasses, bed-straw and milky-pink convolvulus, pale purple scabious and here and there darker valerian. From several places standing on a hedge or looking through a gate, I can glimpse the sea. The sea is there all right, the great Atlantic, emerald green, wrinkled, glittering, sliding streaks of water, spotted dark blue here and there with reflections. It was a full tide, tamed and quiet for the moment, sliding round this inhospitable coast of North Cornwall, with white crescents of surf floating close inshore. From here on these high-up fields, where blackthorn is sliced by the sea wind and leans inland, I can see all along the rocky cliffs to Tintagel Head. Behind me is even grander coast to the Rumps Point and Pentire. Cliffs and ocean are fine to watch from these high, windy fields as cloud shadows race over them. But where can there be a town? Less than half a mile and still no sight of it!

There is no doubt this is the way to approach Port Isaac, from St. Endellion on the Polzeath side of the port. The final hill is very steep and there is only a disused quarry in which you can park a motor car if you are not on foot. Not until you round a corner do you see any sign of Port Isaac at all. Then you see it all, huddled in a steep valley, a cover at the end of a combe, roofs and roofs, tumbling down either steep hillside in a race for shelter from the south-west gales. A fresh-water stream pours brown and cold along the valley, under slate bridges, between old houses, under the road and out into the little harbour.

Port Isaac is Polperro without the self-consciousness, St. Ives without the artists. The same whitewashed slate houses with feathery-looking roofs which have been "grouted"—that is to say the old slates have been cemented over and limewashed—the same narrow airless passages between whitewashed walls. But here are winding paths that climb up steps of beautiful blue-green Delabole slate to other winding paths, hills too steep for anyone with heart trouble to manage, roads and lanes too narrow for buses or coaches. One of the sights of Port Isaac used to be to watch the Life-Boat being brought down Fore Street and missing the walls by inches as she was manœuvred round the bend at the *Golden Lion* into the Town Platt.

Port Isaac has no grand architecture.

A simple slate Methodist chapel and Sunday school in the Georgian tradition hangs over the harbour and is the prettiest building in the town. On the opposite side of the water is a picturesque Gothic style school, from whose pointed windows the teachers could, if they wished, pitch their pupils down the cliff side into the harbour below. Then, lost in rambling cliff paths between the walls, some so narrow that a fat man could not use them, is my favourite house in Port Isaac. It is called the "Birdcage": an irregular pentagon in shape, one small room thick, and three storeys high, and hung on the weather sides with slates which have gone a delicate silvery blue. It's empty now and obviously "condemned." For that is the sad thing about Port Isaac. It is the kind of place Town Planners hate: the quintessence of the quaint. There are no boulevards, no car stands or clinics. The dentist calls once a week and brings his instruments with him in his car.

The Community Centre is all wrong by Town Planning standards. It is not the public-house, but the Liberal Club. Anyone who knows Cornish fishermen must know that most of them do not drink, many are chapel-goers and a Liberal Club without a licence is the sort of place where you would expect to find them.

The trade of Port Isaac really *is* fishing. The harbour does not draw much water. It hardly is a harbour. A better description would be an unexpected cove between high cliffs. Two arms have been built out into the water to keep back the bigger seas, while great guardian headlands keep the harbour calm in most weathers. It is used by small craft and these are reached by dinghies drawn up on the Town Platt among lobster pots and nets. The promise of a dark night after a shoal of pilchards had been sighted, the sound of rowlocks and splashing of oars in harbour water, boarding the fishing boat from the dinghy, the outside roar of the sea, the dark cliffs fading in twilight and dropping away as we move out to open sea, letting down the nets and drifting. Those were the times! Unless, like me, you were a shocking sailor and sick all night and thanking God for the dawn light and the nearing cliffs of Varley Head as you made for home and harbour.

Even if you are no sailor, the smell of fish tells you the chief business of the port. And your eyes will tell you too. For the little houses (the oldest are sixteenth century), though so huddled together and so steeply hung on to cliffs, are like all fishermen's houses, wonderfully clean and polished. Sparkling quartz, known as Cornish Diamond, is cemented into garden walls, figs and fuchsia bushes grow in tiny gardens, big shells from the Orient rest on window sills, brass and paint of front doors shine, carpentry is excellent, and all windows that *can* look out to sea, so that even as they die the old fishermen of Port Isaac may watch the tides. I expect the old people will all soon be moved to some very ugly council houses being built on the windy hilltop in those hideous grey cement things called "Cornish blocks."

Across stupendous cliffs, as full of flowers as a rock garden, is another little fishing port—Port Quin, an empty Port Isaac, mournful and still. For here the old cottages are nearly all ruins; the harbour is deserted, the gardens, once so trim, are grown over with elder and ash saplings, honeysuckle and fennel. The salting sheds are in ruins too. The story is that the whole fishing fleet of the village went down in a gale, and thirty-two women were left widows.

And beyond Port Quin what caves, what rocks, what shuddering heights of striped slate, what hidden beaches and barnacled boulders, what pools where seals bask, there are between here and Pentire Point. All picturesque and grand, as blazing with colour as are the strange rock pools themselves on a summer day. The colours are brighter than the tropics. The veined rock, in which the warm salt water lies, is purple with white lines and then green, then purple again. Warm forests of red seaweed grow there, and green seaweed which looks like elm trees. If there is sand on the bottom of the pool, and the red weed waving, you may see a huge prawn gliding and shooting backwards, and the sudden dash of a small fish, too quick for the eye to see more than the sudden cloud of sand it raises. Or the rock pool may be one with shells and shingle at the bottom and perhaps those rose-tinted cowries, the pearls of this coast, and a huge starfish, magnified by the water in all its pink and grey and purple colouring. Never was such colour, never is the wonder of God's creation more brought home to me than when I see the strange, merciless bright-coloured world of these Cornish rock pools. But in a storm or in a mist how infinitely horrible and mysterious this coast can be, as the rollers smash and suck, the blowholes thunder, and caves syphon out fountains of sea water a hundred feet and more into the air.

> *'Tis harsh to hear from ledge or peak*
> *The cruel cormorants' tuneless shriek*
> *Fierce songs they chant, in pool or cave*
> *Dark wanderers of the Western wave.*

So wrote Hawker the parson poet of Morwenstowe, not many miles higher up the coast. He knew that the sea is an army fighting the land, as do the men of Port Isaac. But I like to stand in summer by the bit of wall in Fore Street, and lean over to look down at the harbour and inland at the little town below me. It is evening, harvest festival time. The small Victorian church has been hung with lobster pots and dressed with crabs and seaweed—a harvest festival of the sea. Church is over, but Chapel is still on. As I stand on this view-point above the town, the sea gulls are crying and wheeling, the flowery cliffs take the evening sun, the silvery slates of the old town turn pale gold. Above the lap of the harbour water, the wail of gulls and thunder of the sea beyond the headlands, comes the final hymn from the Methodist Chapel across the green and gently rolling harbour flood.

Padstow

Some think of the farthest away places as Spitzbergen or Honolulu. But give me Padstow, though I can reach it any day from Waterloo without crossing the sea. For Padstow is in Cornwall and Cornwall is another country. And Padstow is farther away in spirit even than Land's End. It is less touristy than other fishing towns like Polperro and St. Ives: less dramatic than Boscastle or Tintagel: only just not a village, for it has more than two thousand inhabitants. It is an ancient unobvious place, hidden away from the south-west gales below a hill on the sandy estuary of the River Camel. It does not look at the open sea but across the tidal water to the sand-dunes of rock and the famous St. Enodoc Golf Course. There is no beach, only an oily harbour and remarkably large prawns may be netted where the town drains pour into the Camel.

Green Southern Railway engines came right into the brown and cream Great Western district of Cornwall, to reach Padstow. Launceston, Egloskerry, Otterham, Tresmeer, Camelford—and so on, down that windy single line. I know the stations by heart, the slate and granite-built waiting rooms, the oil lamps and veronica bushes, the great Delabole Quarry, the little high-hedged fields, and I know where the small-holdings grow fewer and the fields larger and browner, so that I can see the distant outline of Brown Willy and Rough Tor on Bodmin Moor. Then the train goes fast downhill through high cuttings and a wooded valley. We round a bend and there is the flat marsh of the Camel, there are the little rows of blackish-green cottages along the river at Egloshayle and we are at Wadebridge, next stop Padstow. The next five and a half miles beside the broadening Camel to Padstow. is the most beautiful train journey I know. See it on a fine evening at high tide with golden light on the low hills, the heron-haunted mud coves flooded over, the sudden thunder as we cross the bridge over Little Petherick creek, the glimpses of slate roofs and a deserted jetty among spindly Cornish elms, the wide and unexpected sight of open sea at the river mouth, the huge spread-out waste of water with brown ploughed fields coming down to little cliffs where no waves break but only salt tides ripple up and ebb away. Then the utter endness of the end of the line at Padstow—260 miles of it from London. The smell of fish and seaweed, the crying of gulls and the warm, moist, west country air and valerian growing wild on slate walls.

The approach to Padstow I like most of all is the one I have made ever since I was a child. It is by ferry from the other side of the estuary. It was best in a bit of a sea with a stiff breeze against an incoming tide, puffs of white foam bursting up below the great head of distant Pentire and round the unapproachable cliffs of the rocky island of Newland which seems, from the ferry boat, to stand half-way between Pentire and Stepper Point at the mouth of the river. We would dip our hands in the water and pretend to feel seasick with each heave of the boat and then the town would spread out before us, its slate roofs climbing up the hillside from the wooden wharves of the harbour till they reached the old church tower and the semi-circle of wind-slashed elms which run as a dark belt right around the top of the town, as though to strap the town in more securely still against those south-west gales. Sometimes we would return on a fine, still evening, laden with the week's shopping, and see that familiar view lessen away from the ferry boat while the Padstow Bells, always well rung, would pour their music across the water, reminding me of Parson Hawker's lines—

> *Come to thy God in time!*
> *Thus saith their pealing chime*
> *Youth, Manhood, Old Age past!*
> *Come to thy God at last!*

Padstow is a fishing port and a shopping centre. There is an ice factory, an attractive Georgian Customs House, a hideous post office, an electric light company founded in 1911, and a gas works founded in 1868, this last, beside sad and peeling Public Rooms of yellow stucco dated 1840.

Vast numbers of service people pour in today from a desert that has been made in the neighbouring parishes of St. Eval and St. Merryn—a form of desert known as an aerodrome.

But the chief fact about modern Padstow to interest fact-maniacs, starts with a mermaid. She was combing her hair and singing in the estuary, when a Padstow youth went walking along the cliffs towards the open sea. He shot at her and in her rage she plunged down below the water and picked up a handful of sand which she threw towards Padstow, and that was the start of the Doom Bar. This bar is a bank of sand which for centuries has been slowly silting up the estuary.

In 1948 at a Town Council meeting a letter was read from a Yarmouth firm of ship owners: "We have always been in the habit of sending our boats to Padstow, as we did last year, and we intend to do so again in 1949 during February, March and April. Like everyone else, we are concerned about the silting up of the estuary, making it extremely difficult to manoeuvre our ships in and out of port, and if action is not taken very soon we shall be unable to use the port at all, to our mutual detriment." So there are hundreds of thousands of tons of agricultural silver sand, increasing and increasing. I can well remember how as a child I could see the hulks of ships which had been wrecked on the Doom Bar sticking up black out of the yellow sand.

These are now all covered over. Who will take the sand away? And how will they do it. Miracles are always happening. In Padstow they are easier to believe in than in most places, because it is so ancient a town. So probably the port of Padstow will be saved, even if it is a Government Department that performs the miracle.

Slate-hung houses are built in a semi-circle round the harbour. Here and there the silver-blue tiled buildings are diversified by an old rose-coloured brick house and near me is a building called *The Abbey House*, with granite fifteenth-century quoins. A boy standing up in a dinghy propels her backwards across the calm, oily water by working an oar to and fro in the stern. I turn into the quiet square of the *Ship Hotel* and notice that Miss Tonkin's boot shop is no longer there, though her house with its ferns in the window and lace curtains, its lush, enclosed front and back gardens, still stands. I see that a jeweller's shop has been transformed into a souvenir haunt of tourists and new diamond-leaded panes look odd in the windows, and wooden beams, unknown in Cornwall, are fixed on to the outside walls. The main streets are, thank goodness, little altered. There's not much grand architecture in Padstow. It is all humble unobtrusive houses, three storeys high. Yet as soon as one of them is taken down, the look of the town suffers. I take one of the many narrow roads that lead up the hill. And as I reach the upper air near the church, I realise what a lot of gardens and houses there are in Padstow, though the place looks all slate from the waterside. For here one can look down at the roofs of the houses, on palms and ilex trees and bushes of hydrangeas peeping above slate walls. Narrow public passages pass right through houses under stone arches and lead past high garden walls, down steps under another house to a further street. And I begin to notice that this slate is not grey, as we are inclined to think is all Cornish slate, but a beautiful pale green, streaked here and there with reddish-brown. This is all hewn locally from the cliffs. Slate roofs grouted over with cement and then lime-washed, slate walls,

slate paving stones and, as I near the churchyard gate, slate hedges as
high as a house on either side of me, stuffed with ferns and pennywort.
I saw the little purple flowers of ivy-leaved toadflax on these hedges
blooming as late as November last. Above these stone hedges are
holly bushes and beyond the holly the circling belt of Cornish elms.
A wrought-iron gate opens into the churchyard. In tree-shaded grass
are slate headstones with deep-cut lettering of the eighteenth and early
nineteenth centuries and cherubs with ploughboy faces, Victorian
marble stones to sailors with carved anchors and cables. The parish
church of St. Petroc is built of a brown-grey slate and its large fifteenth-
century windows are crisply carved out of that dark blue-black
Cataclewse stone, a most beautiful hard stone for carving which
lasts the centuries. The church is unusually large and lofty inside for a
Cornish building. It was pleasantly restored in the last century.
A huge monument with kneeling figures painted in reds and whites and
yellows and blacks commemorates Sir Nicholas Prideaux, 1627, and
leads me to Padstow's great house, Prideaux Place.

It stands on a grass clearing among elms, firs and many ilex trees,
that specially west country tree, not far from the church, near the
higher part of the town where late Georgian houses with ilex and palm-
shaded gardens and glass-houses with geraniums and grapes in them,
suggest the land agent, the doctor, retired tradesmen and old sea
captains. A sign saying "No through road" encourages me to walk
through, and I come to a low castellated slate wall in a toy-fort Gothic
style, with a genuine Gothic door of dark-blue Cataclewse stone let
into it. Behind this, in full view of the road, is the E-shaped manor
house. The eastern front looks over the road to its little-planted
park and on to the distant low sand hills across the estuary. The
feathery slate walls are battlemented on top. Over the entrance
porch, in the wings, and in the spaces between them, are noble granite
windows. Even the old lead rain-water heads are there, with the
Prideaux crest and initials on them. A large magnolia shelters in one

fold of the house and a Georgian semi-circular bay is just seen on the south wing, looking across another part of the park. The inside of the house is said to be full of panelling and wood carving and plaster-work and fine furniture.

All this is Elizabethan and seventeenth century. And the church and the houses in the town are medieval or Georgian. They seem comparatively new. What becomes apparent about Padstow is that it is even older than its oldest buildings. When the River Camel was narrower and when woods waved in the estuary which are now covered with sand, thirteen hundred years ago, St. Petroc, Servant of God and son of a Welsh king, crossed the sea from Ireland in a coracle and landed at Trebetherick on the other side of the water. And then he crossed the river and founded a monastery which was known as Petrocstow—that is to say Petroc's church—which we now pronounce Padstow. Many miracles are recorded of him, tales of his kindness to animals, his long prayers standing in a stream on Bodmin moor where to this day his little beehive cell, made of turf and granite, survives. He raised the dead, cured the sick, tamed a savage, serpent-eating monster. A medieval life of St. Petroc was discovered recently which ended thus:

"A woman, feeling thirsty one night, drank water out of a water-jug and swallowed a small serpent (in consequence of which) she was for many years in bad health. As no physicians benefited her, she was brought to the holy man. He made a mixture of water and earth which he gave the sick woman to drink, and immediately she had swallowed it she vomited a serpent three feet long, but dead, and the same hour she recovered her health and gave thanks to god.

"After these and many such like miracles, Blessed Petroc, con-tinually longing for heavenly things, after afflicting his body with much rigour, full of days departed to God, on the day before the nones of June. The sacred body, therefore, worn out with fastings and vigils, is committed to the dust, and the bosom of Abraham receives his spirit, the angels singing to welcome it. At his tomb miracles frequently take place and his bones, albeit dry, retain the power of his virtues. May his glorious merits intercede for us with Christ, Who with the Father liveth and reigneth world without end.   AMEN."

I do not know whether St. Petroc's day, the 4th of June, is still kept in Padstow church; it is in Bodmin parish church and in most of the other thirty or forty churches in Wales, Devon and Cornwall which are dedicated to him.   His cult has survived too in Brittany and at Loperec (Locus Petroci) they have a statue of him, a more lively one than the little stone one in Padstow church.   It shows a benign, bearded man in a spangled cloak, in one hand he holds the gospels and with the other he strokes a thin, nobbly little deer which has jumped up to him and put its forepaws on his breast.   Blessed St. Petroc!   He was the chief of all Cornish saints, a man of pervading gentleness.

St. Petroc may be neglected in Padstow today.   But the Hobby-horse is not.   Whether it came in with the Danes who sacked the town in 981 and drove St. Petroc's monks to Bodmin or whether it was a pagan rite which St. Petroc himself may have witnessed with displeasure, I leave to antiquarians to dispute.   The Padstow Hobby-horse is a folk revival which is almost certainly of pagan origin. Moreover, it is as genuine and unselfconscious as the Morris Dancing at Bampton-in-the-Bush, Oxfordshire, and not even broadcasting it or an influx of tourists will take the strange and secret character from the ceremonies connected with it.   For this is what happens.   On the day before May Day, green boughs are put up against the houses.   And that night every man and woman in Padstow is awake with excitement. I knew someone who was next to a Padstow man in the trenches in the 1914 war.   On the night before May Day, the Padstow man became so excited he couldn't keep still.   The old 'obby 'oss was mounting in his blood and his mates had to hold him back from jumping over the top and dancing about in No-man's-land.

Now imagine a still night, the last of April, the first of May. Starlight above the chimney pots. Moon on the harbour. Moonlight shadows of houses on opposite slate walls. At about two in the morning the song begins. Here are the words.

> *With a merry ring and with the joyful spring,*
> *For summer is a-come unto day*
> *How happy are those little birds which so merrily do sing*
> *In the merry morning of May.*

Then the men go round to the big houses of the town singing below the windows a variety of verses—

> *"Arise up Mr. Brabyn I know you well afine*
> *You have a shilling in your purse and I wish it were in mine."*

And then on to a house where a young girl lives—

> *"Arise up Miss Lobb all in your smock of silk*
> *And all your body under as white as any milk."*

Morning light shines on the water and the green-grey houses. Out on the quay comes the Hobby-horse—it used to be taken for a drink to a pool a mile away from the town. It is a man in a weird mask, painted red and black and white, and he wears a huge hooped skirt made of black tarpaulin which he is meant to lift up, rushing at the ladies to put it over one of their heads. The skirt used to have soot in it. A man dances with the Hobby-horse carrying a club. Suddenly, at about 11.30 in the morning, there is a pause. The Hobby-horse bows down to the ground. The attendant lays his club on its head and the day song begins, a dirge-like strain.

> *"Oh where is St. George? Oh where is he, O?*
> *He's down in his long boat. All on the salt sea, O."*

Then up jumps the Hobby-horse, loud shriek the girls, louder sings the crowd and wilder grows the dance—

> *With a merry ring and with a joyful spring*
> *For summer is a-come unto day*
> *How happy are those little birds which so merrily do sing*
> *In the merry morning of May.*

Ilfracombe

Ilfracombe is the end of everything.   The express train had only three carriages left which had wound so long and crowded out of Waterloo.   Parts of it had been dropped off at Exeter and Barnstaple. Here at Ilfracombe staion, the end of the line, we seemed to hang in air on a cliff top, with the town two hundred feet below us and silvery slate cliffs, sea and the far-seen coast of Wales beyond.

It was hard to believe there was going to be a town after all those miles of bleak North Devon fields with their high stone hedges, black thorns, foxgloves and hardly a house in sight.   There might perhaps be a village, quite a big village, but not a town.   Ilfracombe seems enormous. It has several churches, lines of Welsh-looking lodging houses, hills and valleys filled with houses, shops, cinemas and loud speakers giving off crooning.   It is the Blackpool of the West, the Douglas of North Devon, the noise and the glitter dazzled me at first so that I could not sort out Ilfracombe nor discover why it had ever been built and if it had to be in North Devon, why not at some more spectacular place like Heddon's Mouth or Lynton where Exmoor rises to nearly a thousand feet and cascades in rocks and bracken to the Bristol Channel?   Why is Ilfracombe *here* where there is no sand and these great hills, grass on the landward side, slate on the seaward, hide much of the town from the sea?

I went up Torrs Walks and from 450 feet looked back on the town. My son and I set off in a speed boat swirling past the caves and cliffs to glimpse between the gaps in spray and rock the terraces of the town. Leaving him to take more trips on the speed boat, I climbed to airy suburbs where boarding houses flew bathing dresses from upstairs windows. I visited the Museum, quite the nicest and most old-fashioned provincial museum I have ever seen, crowded with all sorts of objects; old tickets, stuffed crocodiles, heathen gods, local photographs and prints and playbills, butterflies, moths and birds, seaweed arranged to look like flowers and feathers arranged to look like fruit. Indeed, this Museum must be almost the last unspoiled one left in England. It has no horn-rimmed experts in it cataloguing and killing things with their erudition and asking you not to touch.

From walks and drives and cruises, and chiefly from this Museum, I began to piece together the growth of Ilfracombe. It is an epitome of seaside history, and this must be the kind of way it grew. Until a hundred and fifty years ago nobody cared about living by the sea, unless they were fishermen or sailors. Then, Ilfracombe consisted of a harbour naturally guarded by Lantern Hill, on the top of which is an old chapel of St. Nicholas, possibly Celtic in origin. Nearly a mile further up the brook which poured into the harbour were an old village and parish church. In that large and graceful church today you can feel the old West Country Ilfracombe about you, for it is a singularly countrified church for so large a town. It has carved barrel roofs of wood; it has wall tablets and low West-Country style columns. And not far off are old houses with slate-hung sides, yellow stucco fronts and Georgian windows. In a place called Cuddeford's Passage, off the High Street, I found Clovelly-like cottages built of slate and whitewashed. This is all genuine Devon.

In Georgian days the harbour was extended. Ilfracombe grew as a fishing port. Then in about 1830 someone saw its possibilities as a watering place. Mild, warm, almost as sunny as Nice, it was a fuchsia-shaded ilex-waving paradise. Indeed, the poet Charles Abraham Elton of Clevedon thus described it in 1835—

> *Thy craggy coves, O Ilfracombe!*
> *The outline of thy ridgy hills,*
> *The ash-tree dell's sun quivering gloom,*
> *And pebbled dash of viewless rills.*

Many attractive Georgian houses were built above the harbour and set snugly down in the grassy valley between harbour and church. Still later, this mild climate and these mildly beetling rocks, not *too* rugged and wild, these well-spoken Devon sailors round the little harbour—all were just the thing for Mid-Victorian merchants and their families. So next came stupendous hotels erected in the turfy hollow, St. Pancras Station in white brick, the Louvre in red and white bricks. These hotels are the most impressive buildings in the place and the most prominent is the Ilfracombe Hotel built in 1867 in the French Gothic style in coloured bricks.

Since those Mid-Victorian days, Ilfracombe has changed in character. Rich West Country and London merchants ceased to come. The Welsh arrived by steamer from Barry, Swansea and Cardiff; the railway opened in 1874 and made the journey less adventurous and the place less what used to be called "exclusive". So the combe filled up not with noble isolated villas proclaiming the riches of their occupants, but with large hotels and rows upon rows of boarding houses designed to cram bedrooms into the smallest possible space. Ilfracombe became what it still is, the people's playground.

My last picture of Ilfracombe is not of sea, nor of Devon but of that peculiar and exotic thing known as "seaside". I stand on a steep hill on the way to the station. Warm salty air is round me and I can smell the Atlantic but cannot see it. There rises in front of me a row of late Victorian boarding houses in shiny yellow brick, relieved with shiny red, a style very popular in Ilfracombe. The roofs are of blue slate and red tiles pick out the ridges. The cast-iron railings are painted silver and the garden behind them is bright with lobelias, geraniums and hydrangeas. A palm tree rises as high as the first floor window. The piers of the front gate are topped with pieces of white quartz. Ilfracombe, with your chapels, evangelical churches, chars-à-bancs and variegated terraces, long may you lie embedded in your gorgeous cliffs and hills! Nature made you lovely. Man has

227

not improved you. But on a sunny summer evening you are lovely still.

Clevedon

Clevedon has the most character, the widest diversity of scenery, the fewest really hideous buildings of all the "seaside" places I have lately visited. It is quiet, mild, medium-sized. Its churches are full, its shops are polite, the same families come to it year after year, the same type of people who like peace and who mistrust so-called "progress" walk along its ilex-shaded roads. Upon that slender cast-iron pier, built in 1869, strode T. E. Brown, the Clifton schoolmaster and poet. Here he composed a poem about the salmon rushing up the Severn from the sea. To Clevedon, the body of Arthur Hallam was brought in 1833—

> *The Danube to the Severn gave*
> *The darken'd heart that beat no more;*
> *They laid him by the pleasant shore,*
> *And in the hearing of the wave.*
>
> *There twice a day the Severn fills,*
> *The salt sea-water passes by,*
> *And hushes half the babbling Wye*
> *And makes a silence in the hills.*

Not thirty years earlier Coleridge had brought his young bride to Clevedon to a small cottage which still survives:

> *Low was our pretty cot: our tallest rose*
> *Peeped at the chamber window. We could hear*
> *At silent noon, and eve and early morn*
> *The sea's faint murmur.*

Now he would hear only bus engines, for a big garage is opposite to the cottage where he lived.

Great writers have come to Clevedon ever since the Elton family bought Clevedon Court in Queen Anne's reign. Successive Eltons who seem always to have been men of taste and vision, improved the town throughout the last century, Clevedon Court where the Eltons still live is said to be the oldest inhabited house in England. Most of what one sees from the Bristol road looks Tudor, Jacobean and later, but parts of it go back to Edward II. Terraced gardens rise to oak and ilex, beech and ash woods. These form a dark and satisfying background to the house which is of honey-coloured and silvery lime-stone, battlemented and irregular.

Much of Clevedon looks as though it were a continuation of the private park of the Court, thanks to skilful planting and planning in Victorian times. Roads wind among trees, there is plenty of open space. Skylines are often left undisturbed by building. Elton Road and Hallam Road leave little doubt about who the original owners were. Albert, Victoria and Alexandra roads give one a good idea of the dates of others. The earliest development is to be found in simple late Georgian houses of stucco washed cream or white and set down below the crest of Dial Hill, where they peep from myrtle bushes and ilex trees. What a comment on our civilisation it is that these modest houses actually *beautify* the hillside, while a few yards above them, a row of pre-war villas, commanding fine views no doubt, ruin the sky-line for miles with their shapelessness and alien red brick among all this silvery stone. Such vandalism would never have been allowed under the benevolent liberalism of Elton control. The prevalent style of house in the older, mid-Victorian parts of Clevedon is Gothic or Italianate, built of local greyish-blue stone, sometimes flecked with pink or honey-yellow. Bargeboards adorn gables, roofs are slated, trees surround lawns and hang over garden walls. It is all as though many comfortable vicarages had been set down here among trees within sound of the sea. Well-designed Victorian lamp posts, instead of boa constrictors in concrete, adorn the streets. Walks and shelters and flowering shrubs and parks decorate the sea front. Only the sea itself is a bit of a failure.   It is often muddy with that chocolate mud one sees at Weston and which seems to clog the waves and dye their thin tops a pinky-brown.   This mud lies upon the rocks.   Bathing in the marine lake at Clevedon I accidentally touched some with my toe— it had the feeling of a dead body.

But stand on Castle Hill three hundred feet above the town, in the octagonal ruin of Stuart times called Walton Castle, and view the landscape round.   The gables of Clevedon rise from the spur of hills below us.   Clifton is only twelve miles away behind us.   Backbones of hill leading home to Bristol are dark with waving woods.   Beyond the town towards Weston run flat and pale green moors till they meet the blue outline of the Mendips like the background of a Flemish stained-glass window.   The Bristol Channel is a bronze shield streaked with sunlight.   Flat Holm and Steep Holm are outlined to the west, and to the north the coast of South Wales stretches out of sight.   What was a tidal river has become a huge dividing sea.   This wonderful view from Castle Hill is all Georgian enjoyment of the picturesque, especially when seen through an ivy-mantled arch.

But at the other end of the town, where the old parish church stands sheltered between two grassy hills at the sea's edge, the atmosphere is older and even Celtic.   The cruciform church built of dark grey slate, with storm-resisting central tower, the windy churchyard, the low bushes blown landward, the brown grass, cliff plants and nearby thud and thunder of water, all make me think I am in Cornwall.

Clevedon is saved by being on the way to nowhere.   The dear old light railway which connected it with Portishead has been ripped up by modern progress, which here means buses.   But buses don't go with Clevedon, any more than do modernistic arcades of shops and the new Post Office at the cross roads in the town.   Now only a Great Western branch from Yatton serves the town.   Let the chars-à-bancs and megaphones and multitudes roar down distant main roads to Weston and to Cheddar Gorge.   Clevedon will then still be left as it is, a civilised

and decorative seaside town, shunned, thank heaven, by modern barbarism, a refuge in time of trouble, a beautiful haven of quiet.

Highworth

I have never seen Highworth given due praise in guide books for
what it is—one of the most charming and unassuming country towns in
the West of England. It is unspoiled by the vulgar fascias of chain
stores, concrete lamp posts don't lean above its houses like seasick
giants spewing orange light at night that turns us all to corpses, the
roaring hideousness of main roads has left Highworth undisturbed.
The only ugly things about it are some fussy red modern villas on the
outskirts and too many electric light and telegraph wires zig-zagging
across its High Street.

Highworth is extraordinary because it has more beautiful buildings
than it has ugly ones. It is mostly a Cotswold-coloured place of pale
grey stone gathered round its church high on a hill, with a High Street
and Market Place, a street at right angles, a Georgian doctor's house in
red brick with a fine white wooden porch and doorway, and one more
grand brick house—and these Georgian brick houses look as beautiful
and ripe as autumn apples among all this silver stone of the streets.

Then Highworth is full of old inns with bay windows and swinging
signs and arches for coaches to go under into cobbled yards; there is a
pleasant late Georgian Congregational church; wistaria and vines trail
over some of the houses; high garden walls show glimpses of fruit trees
rising above them. It would not surprise me to see periwigged men in
knee breeches and ladies in silks and countrymen in smocks walking
about in Sheep Street and in High Street or down Vicarage Lane,
Highworth. They would not look out of place.

Even the Matting Factory is tucked away out of sight. So is the
church. You can see its tower everywhere but you have to look
through an arch under a house in the High Street to glimpse the porch
and lime-shaded churchyard. The church has a fine painted Royal

Arms, a huge parish chest with three padlocks, some Norman work and much later work and much too much late-Victorian work.

Highworth is on the border of the West Country and the Midlands, and to me it is the *centre* of some of the loveliest country round its feet—Coleshill House in Berkshire, that four-square masterpiece of stone built in Charles II's reign with its lantern and moulded chimneys rising mightily from surrounding elms; Great Coxwell barn, the oldest and grandest tithe barn in Britain, beating, in my opinion, those at Abbotsbury in Dorset and Harmondsworth in Middlesex; Inglesham church down by the Thames, the church which William Morris saved from so-called restoration—there it is, clear glass, box pews, old screens and wall paintings, a stoney, lichen-crusted country church among the whispering grasses. These are some of the sights of the country round Highworth. Countless unknown lanes lead up the hill to Highworth.

When I am abroad and want to recall a typically English town, I think of Highworth. It is the sort of town read about in novels from *Cranford* to Miss MacNaughten. Ah, Highworth as a whole! Churches and chapels, doctors' houses, Vicarage, walled gardens with pears and plums, railway station, inns and distant cemetery, old shops and winding streets. We walked down one of those narrow lanes, between garden walls, that lead under archways into the High Street. (The only way to see a town is to go down every alley and see the *backs* of the houses.) Ivy-leaved toadflax with its little purple flowers hung over the stone, an uneven line of stone-tiled roofs and slate roofs, stone and brick chimney stacks, leaded windows under eaves, all these formed a base for the church tower. There was a sound of tea being cleared away in a cottage just near us. And suddenly with a burst the bells of Highworth church rang out for Evening Service. As though called by the bells, the late sun burst out and bathed the varied roofs with gold and scooped itself into the uneven panes of old windows. Sun and stone and old brick and garden flowers and church bells. That was Sunday evening in Highworth. That was England.

INDEX

Index

A

Aberdeen, Scottish architecture and classic architects, 21–3; granite, 23–4; three periods of architecture, 25–9

Ackermann's Repository of the Arts, 14, 16–17

Adam brothers, The, 23

Adam, Robert, 63–4

Aidé, Hamilton, 200

Albert, Prince, 190; Memorial, 50, 52, 149

Aldersgate Station, 76

Alexandra Palace Exhibition, 1873, 70

Allingham, William, 199

All Saints' Church, Basingstoke, 139; Margaret Street, London, 137, 154–5; Notting Hill, 138; Tooting, 139

Alum Bay, Isle of Wight, 193–4

Annand, Rupert, 189 n.

Architecture, Scottish and classic architects 21–3; author's preference for first quarter of 19th century, 50–1; antiquarian prejudice and domestic, 51, 57–9; ecclesiastical, 51–5; monumental, 51, 56–7; planning, 51, 59–60; U.S.S.R., 57; jazz modern reaction, 60–1; champions of antiquity, experts, 61–2;

Architecture—*continued*

research worker, 62–3; authority given to antiquarian research, 63–4; position of modern architect, 64–6; entertainment buildings, impermanence of, 67–71, 74; "battle of the styles," 80–1, 124–9, 134, 178; Georgian, 132, 134, 202–5; comparison between domestic of 18th and 19th centuries, 163; classic survival, 135, 145–6; Gothic revival, 128–30, 135–41, 146–9; "hards," 137–8, 152–9; Ruskinian Gothic, 152; *see* also Boggleton, Nonconformist and Victorian

Art Nouveau movement, 130 & n., 141, 174

Arts and Crafts, *see* Morris Movement

Ashbee, 65

Ashmolean, Oxford, 135

Assembly Rooms, Cheltenham, 18–19

Assize Courts, Manchester, 159

B

Bailey's *New Hand-Book for Cheltenham*, 18–19 & n.

Baillie Scott, H., 44, 65, 140, 166

Baker Street Station, 85

Balliol College, Oxford, 159

Balmoral, 29

Index